Charles F. Deems

Coronation Hymns and Songs

For Praise and Prayer Meetings, home and social singing

Charles F. Deems

Coronation Hymns and Songs
For Praise and Prayer Meetings, home and social singing

ISBN/EAN: 9783337181536

Printed in Europe, USA, Canada, Australia, Japan

Cover: Foto ©Lupo / pixelio.de

More available books at **www.hansebooks.com**

CORONATION HYMNS

AND

SONGS:

FOR

PRAISE AND PRAYER MEETINGS,

HOME AND SOCIAL SINGING.

CHARLES F. DEEMS, D.D., LL.D. } Editors.
THEODORE E. PERKINS,

A. S. BARNES & COMPANY:

New York, Chicago & New Orleans.

1879.

COPYRIGHT, 1879, BY A. S. BARNES & CO.

WHY THIS BOOK?

ANOTHER hymn book! Is there any reason for its existence? Yes. Some hymns wear out. While that process is going on, other hymns are produced. From time to time books must be published, embracing those hymns that do not wear out, and giving those that are coming into existence. On the theory of "the survival of the fittest," some will appear in each succeeding book. The others will drop back. The singing public will select. There is no appeal from their verdict.

In this little book we believe will be found *more* hymns that the world will not suffer to die, and more *new* hymns that deserve trial than in any other book extant. If we did not so believe we would not publish. In our opinion, therefore, it is the best book of the kind *now* for sale in Christendom. Ten years hereafter, any one *may* be able to produce one more acceptable: perhaps the present compilers may. We have not been able to find or produce a better. Trusting that this collection may minister to the pleasure and profit of thousands, we present it, in the name of our Master, trusting we have His approval!

AND, "LET ALL THE PEOPLE PRAISE HIM."

[Most of the Hymns and tunes in this work are copyright property, and can only be used by permission first obtained from the Authors or Publishers.]

CORONATION SONGS.

No. 1.   CORONATION. C. M.

Rev. E. PERRONET, 1780.   O. HOLDEN, 1793.

1. All hail the power of Je-sus' name! Let an-gels prostrate fall:
Bring forth the roy-al dia-a-dem, And crown Him Lord of all;
Bring forth the roy-al di-a-dem, And crown Him Lord of all.

2. Crown him, ye mar-tyrs of our God, Who from the Al-tar call;
Ex-tol the stem of Jes-se's rod, And crown Him Lord of all;
Ex-tol the stem of Jesse's rod, And crown Him Lord of all.

3.
Ye chosen seed of Israel's race,
  Ye ransomed from the fall,
Hail him who saves you by his grace,
  And crown him—Lord of all.

4.
Sinners, whose love can ne'er forget
  The wormwood and the gall,
Go, spread your trophies at his feet,
  And crown him—Lord of all.

5.
Let every kindred, every tribe
  On this terrestrial ball,
To him all majesty ascribe,
  And crown him—Lord of all.

6.
Oh that with yonder sacred throng,
  We at his feet may fall;
We'll join the everlasting song,
  And crown him—Lord of all.

No. 2. OH, TO BE READY.

CHARLES F. DEEMS. THEODORE E. PERKINS.

1. Oh to be ready, read-y, Yielding my Saviour my all;

D.C. Oh, to be ready, read-y, Yielding my Saviour my all;

And waiting, with loving patience, For the Master's gracious call:

And waiting, with loving patience, For the Master's gracious call.

Soothing the poor in their sorrow, And helping the rich in their woe;

D.C. for Chorus.

Seek-ing to find new treasures, On suffering Saints to be-stow.

2 Oh, to be ready, ready,
Hidden from every delight,
And hearing no voices of praises,
While toiling alone in the night;
Lonely, unmourned, and forsaken,
And cast from the hearts of all men;
Walking the fiery furnace,
Or sleeping with beasts in their den.

3 Oh, to be ready, ready,
Following the lead of my Lord;
While armed with salvation's helmet,
And the Spirit's flaming sword:
Meeting the foe with high courage,
And fighting the good fight of faith;
Shouting in triumph while dying,
And soaring to life over death.

Copyright, 1879, by Theodore E. Perkins.

No. 3. LOVE OF JESUS.
THEODORE E. PERKINS.

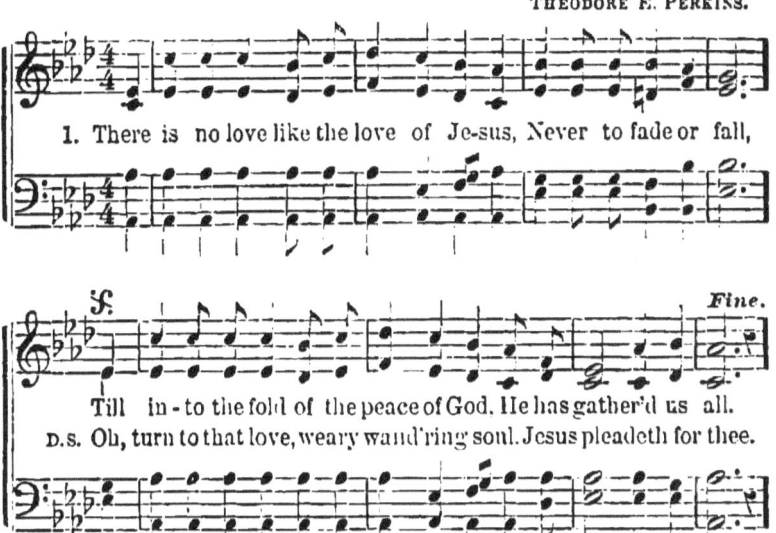

2 There is no heart like the heart of Jesus,
  Filled with a tender love;
  No throb nor throe that our hearts can know,
  But He feels it above.—Cho.

3 There is no eye like the eye of Jesus,
  Piercing so far away;
  Ne'er out of the sight of its tender light
  Can the wanderer stray.—Cho.

4 There is no voice like the voice of Jesus,
  Tender and sweet its chime,
  Like musical ring of the flowing spring
  In the bright summer time.—Cho.

5 Oh, let us hark to the voice of Jesus,
  Oh, may we never roam,
  Till safe we rest on His loving breast,
  In the dear heavenly home.—Cho.

From "Songs of Salvation," by per.

TELL ME MORE ABOUT JESUS.—CONCLUDED.

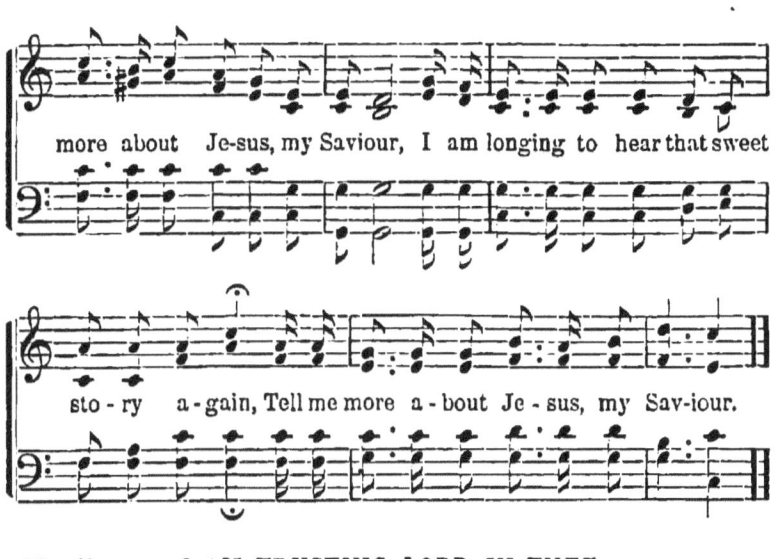

No. 5.   I AM TRUSTING, LORD, IN THEE.
Rev. WM. McDONALD.   WM. G. FISCHER, by per.

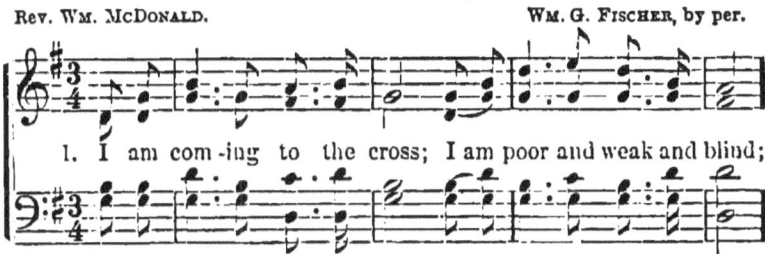

1. I am com-ing to the cross; I am poor and weak and blind;

CHO.—I am trust-ing, Lord, in thee, Dear Lamb of Cal-va-ry;

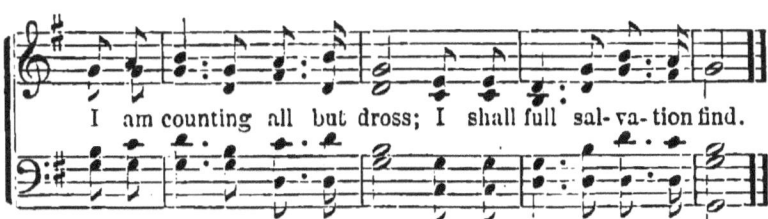

I am counting all but dross; I shall full sal-va-tion find.

Humbly at thy cross I bow, Save me, Je-sus, save me now.

2.
Long my heart has sighed for thee;
Long has evil reigned within;
Jesus sweetly speaks to me,
I will cleanse thee from all sin.

3.
In thy promises I trust;
Now I feel the blood applied;
I am prostrate in the dust.
I with Christ am crucified. (7)

No. 6. REJOICE AND BE GLAD.
Rev. HORATIUS BONAR, 1874.
English Melody.

2 Rejoice and be glad!
  It is sunshine at last!
The clouds have departed,
  The shadows are past.

3 Rejoice and be glad!
  For the blood hath been shed;
Redemption is finished,
  The price hath been paid.

REJOICE AND BE GLAD. (CONCLUDED.)

4 Rejoice and be glad!
　Now the pardon is free!
　The Just for the unjust
　Has died on the tree. *Cho.*

5 Rejoice and be glad!
　For the Lamb that was slain,
　O'er death is triumphant,
　And liveth again. *Cho.*

6 Rejoice and be glad!
　For our King is on high,
　He pleadeth for us on
　His throne in the sky. *Cho.*

7 Rejoice and be glad!
　For He cometh again;
　He cometh in glory,
　The Lamb that was slain.
　　　　　　　　　Cho.

No. 6. 2d Hymn.　REVIVE US AGAIN.

1　We praise Thee, O God! for the Son of Thy love,
　　For Jesus who died, and is now gone above.
Cho.—Hallelujah! Thine the glory, Hallelujah! amen,
　　Hallelujah! Thine the glory, revive us again.

2　We praise Thee, O God! for Thy Spirit of light,
　　Who has shown us our Saviour, and scattered our night.—*Cho.*

3　All glory and praise to the Lamb that was slain,
　　Who has borne all our sins, and cleansed every stain.—*Cho.*

4　All glory and praise to the God of all grace,
　　Who has bought us, and sought us, and guided our ways.—*Cho.*

5　Revive us again; fill each heart with Thy love,
　　May each soul be kindled with fire from above.—*Cho.*
　　　　　　　　　　　　　　　Rev. Wm. Paton Mackey, 1866.

No. 7.　COME TO JESUS TO-DAY.

2 He will save you, &c.
3 Oh, believe Him, &c.
4 He'll receive you, &c.
5 Flee to Jesus, &c.
6 He will hear you, &c.
7 He'll have mercy, &c.
8 He'll forgive you, &c.
9 He will cleanse you, &c.
10 Jesus loves you, &c.

No. 8. PASS NOT BY.

Mrs. E. C. Kinney. T. E. Perkins.

1. Je-sus, Sav-iour, hear our cry! Pass not by, oh, pass not by! Thou art com-ing, Lord, so nigh, Bless us too, oh, pass not by! Lord, ful-fill Thy promise now; Pour Thy Spir-it while we bow; Turn to us, as one we cry, Pass not by, oh, pass not by!

2. We have heard Thy footsteps near, Pass not by, oh, pass not by! See the con-trite sinner's tear—Listen to the longing sigh: Je-sus, hear our earn-est call, Let Thy bless-ing rest on all; When Thy Spir-it is so nigh, Pass not by, oh, pass not by!

3 Prostrate in Thy path we lie—
Pass not by, oh, pass not by!
Lest our very faith should die,
Pass not by, oh, pass not by!
To Thy garments we will cling,
All our need before Thee bring;
Son of David, hear our cry!
Pass not by, oh, pass not by!

4 Lord, we cannot let Thee go,
Pass not by, oh, pass not by!
In our midst Thy presence show,
Till Thou bless us will we cry:
Breathe, oh, breathe on us, we pray:
Tarry not, oh, come to-day,
While we wait, and watch, and cry,
Pass not by, oh, pass not by!

Copyright, 1879, by Theodore E. Perkins.

No. 9. I AM, COMING LORD.

Rev. L. Hartsough.   Hartsough, by per.

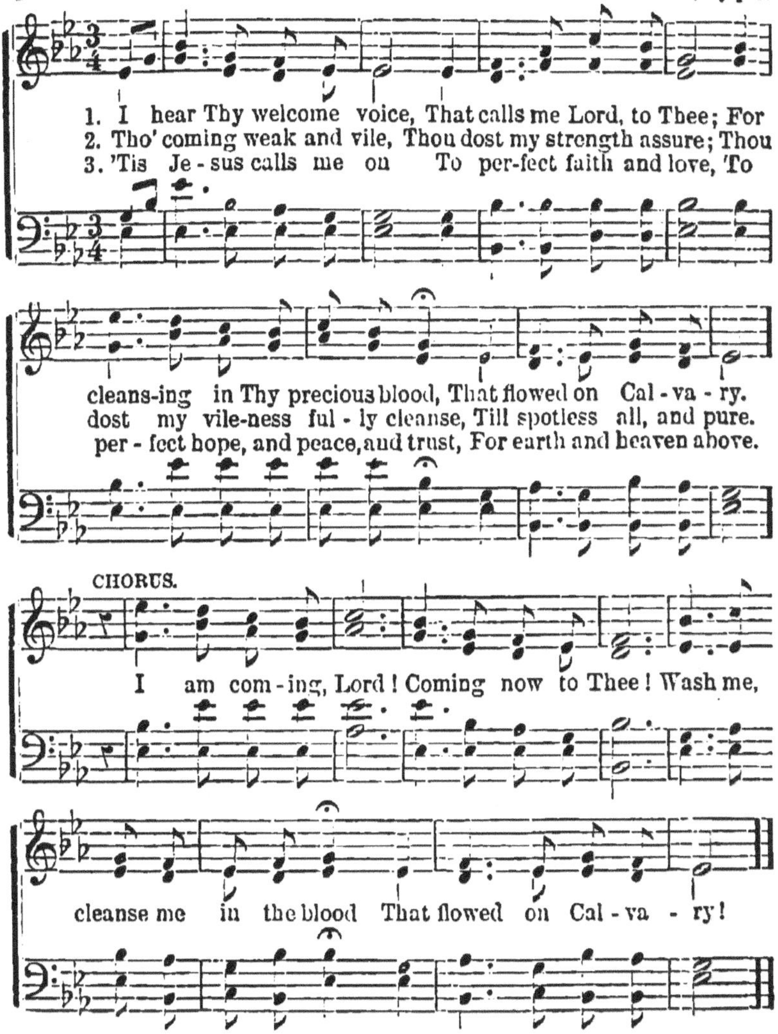

1. I hear Thy welcome voice, That calls me Lord, to Thee; For cleans-ing in Thy precious blood, That flowed on Cal-va-ry.
2. Tho' coming weak and vile, Thou dost my strength assure; Thou dost my vile-ness ful-ly cleanse, Till spotless all, and pure.
3. 'Tis Je-sus calls me on To per-fect faith and love, To per-fect hope, and peace, and trust, For earth and heaven above.

CHORUS.

I am com-ing, Lord! Coming now to Thee! Wash me, cleanse me in the blood That flowed on Cal-va-ry!

4 And He the witness gives
  To loyal hearts and free,
That every promise is fulfilled,
  If faith but brings the plea.—*Cho.*

5 All hail! atoning blood!
  All hail! redeeming grace!
All hail! the gift of Christ, our Lord,
  Our Strength and Righteousness.—*Cho.*

No. 10. CLOSE TO THEE.

FANNY J. CROSBY.   S. J. VAIL, by per.

1. Thou my ev - er-last-ing portion, More than friend or life to me,
2. Not for ease or worldly pleasure, Nor for fame my prayer shall be;
3. Lead me thro' the vale of shadows, Bear me o'er life's fit - ful sea:

All a-long my pilgrim journey, Sav-iour let me walk with Thee.
Glad-ly will I toil and suf-fer, On - ly let me walk with Thee.
Then the gate of life e - ter - nal, May I en - ter, Lord, with Thee.

CHORUS.

Close to Thee, close to Thee, Close to Thee, close to Thee; All a -
Close to Thee, close to Thee, Close to Thee, close to Thee; Glad-ly
Close to Thee, close to Thee, Close to Thee, close to Thee; Then the

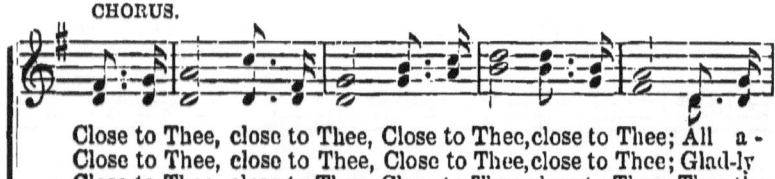

long my pil - grim jour-ney, Sav-iour, let me walk with Thee.
will I toil and suf - fer, On - ly let me walk with Thee.
gate of life e - ter - nal, May I en - ter, Lord, with Thee.

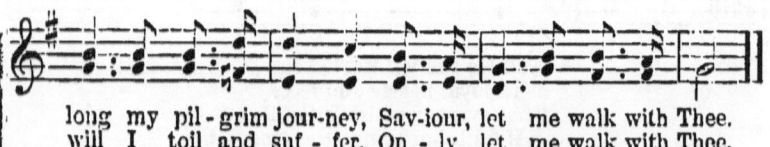

No. 11. THERE IS A FOUNTAIN.
WM. COWPER. WESTERN MELODY.

1. There is a fountain, fill'd with blood, Drawn from Immanuel's veins;
2. The dying thief rejoiced to see That fountain in his day;

And sinners plung'd beneath that flood, Lose all their guilty stains,
And there may I, though vile as he, Wash all my sins a-way,

Lose all their guilt-y stains, Lose all their guilty stains, And
Wash all my sins a-way, Wash all my sins a-way, And

sin-ners plunged beneath that flood Lose all their guilt-y stains.
there may I, tho' vile as he, Wash all my sins a-way.

3.
E'er since by faith I saw the stream
Thy flowing wounds supply,
Redeeming love has been my theme
And shall be till I die.

4.
Then in a nobler, sweeter song
I'll sing thy power to save,
When this poor, lisping, stammering
Lies silent in the grave. [tongue

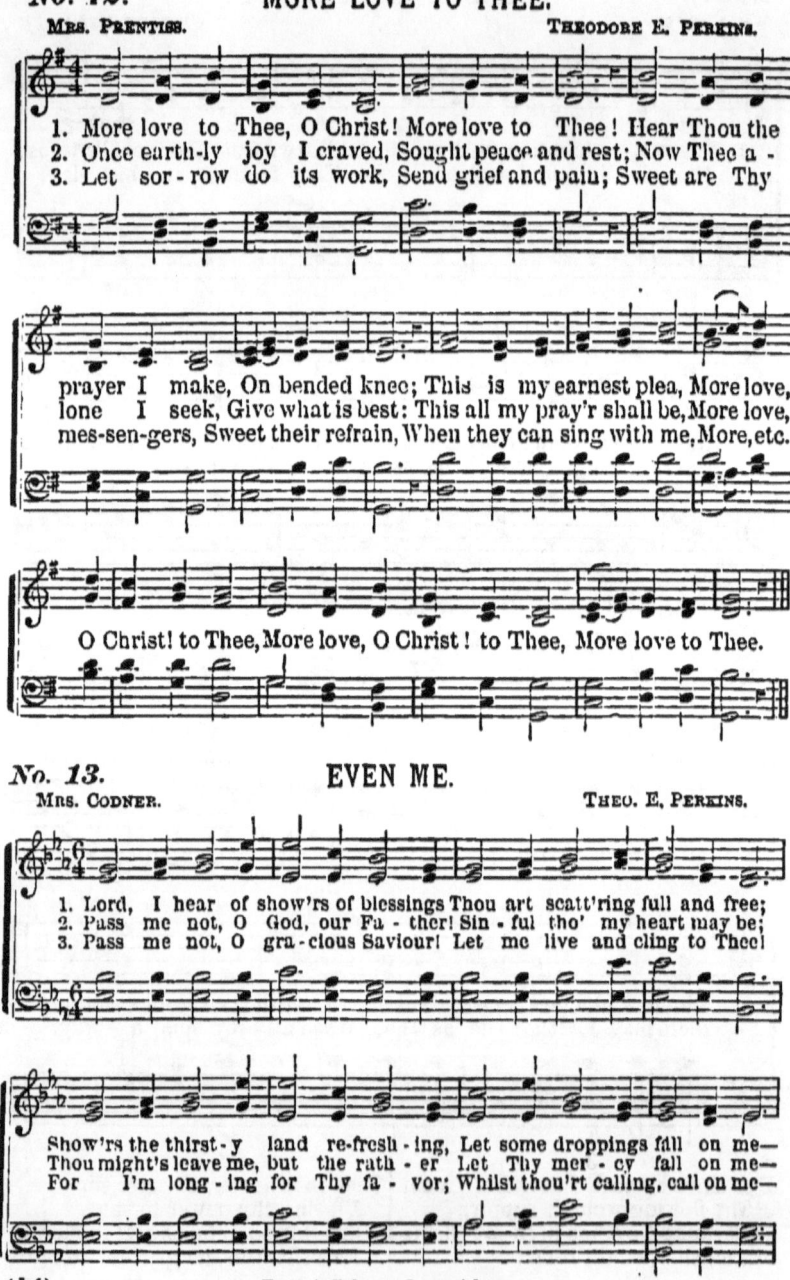

EVEN ME.—CONCLUDED.

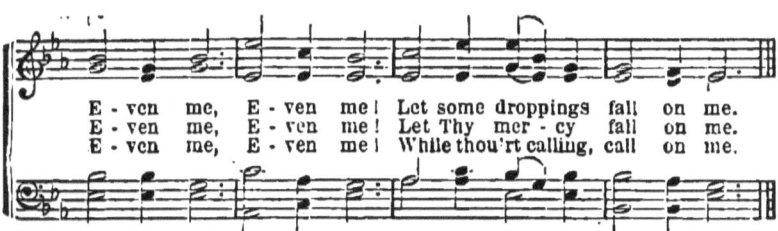

E-ven me, E-ven me! Let some droppings fall on me.
E-ven me, E-ven me! Let Thy mer-cy fall on me.
E-ven me, E-ven me! While thou'rt calling, call on me.

4 Pass me not, O mighty Spirit,
  Thou canst make the blind to see;
  Testify of Jesus' merit!
  Speak some word of power to me.
  Even me, even me !
  Speak some word of power to me.

5 Love of God—so pure and changeless,
  Blood of Christ—so rich, so free;
  Grace of God—so strong and boundless,
  Magnify it all in me !
  Even me, even me !
  Magnify it all in me !

No. 14. JESUS WILL COME.

THEODORE E. PERKINS.

1. How bright that bless-ed hope! Je-sus will come! Let us our
2. Him eve-ry eye shall see, Je-sus will come! Bright will the
3. Full of this bless-ed hope! Je-sus will come! Let us the

heads lift up, Je-sus will come! Morn-ing so bright and clear,
glo-ry be, Je-sus will come! Soon shall the trumpet speak,
cross take up, Je-sus will come! Hap-py re-proach to bear,

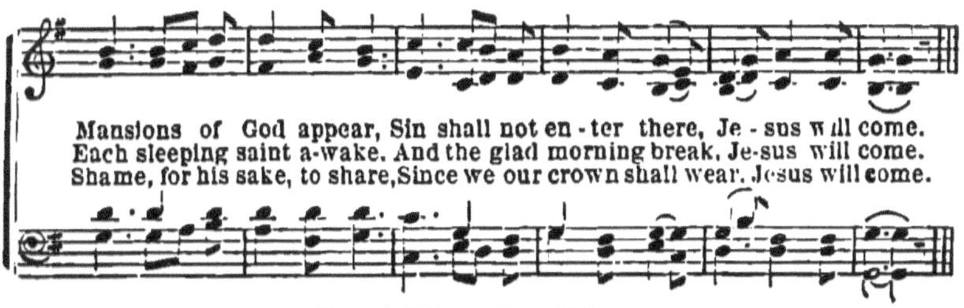

Mansions of God appear, Sin shall not en-ter there, Je-sus will come.
Each sleeping saint a-wake, And the glad morning break, Jesus will come.
Shame, for his sake, to share, Since we our crown shall wear, Jesus will come.

From "Calvary Songs," by per.

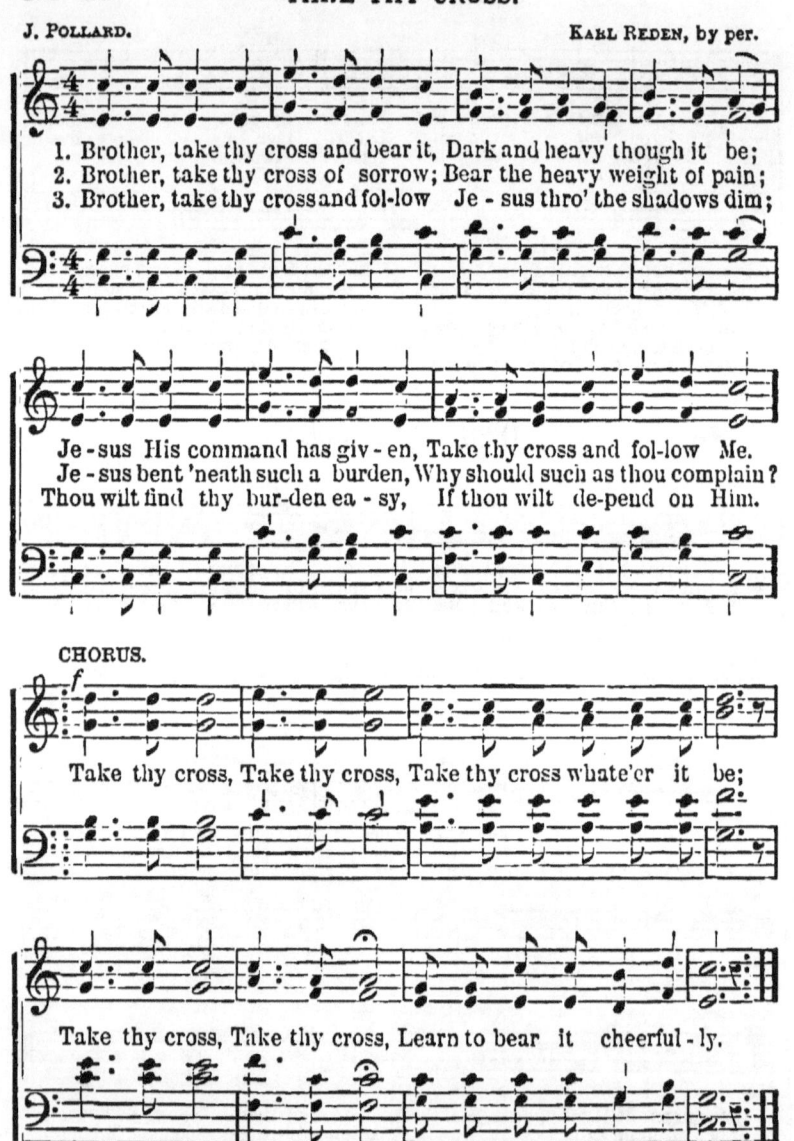

4 Brother, take thy cross; for Jesus
    Gives thee strength its weight to bear;
    Trust Him in the time of sorrow,
    He will hear and answer prayer.—*Cho.*

No. 16. THE LORD WILL PROVIDE.

Mrs. M. A. W. Cook. From "Hallowed Songs," by per.

1. In some way or other the Lord will pro-vide: It may not be
my way, It may not be *thy* way; And yet, in His *own* way, "The
Lord will pro-vide."

2. At some time or other the Lord will pro-vide: It may not be
my time, It may not be *thy* time; And yet, in His *own* way, "The
Lord will pro-vide."

CHORUS.
Then, we'll trust in the Lord, And He will pro-vide; Yes, we'll trust in the Lord, And He will pro-vide.

3 Despond, then, no longer;
The Lord will provide;
And this be the token—
No word He hath spoken
Was ever yet broken:
"The Lord will provide."

4 March on, then, right boldly;
The sea shall divide:
The pathway made glorious,
With shoutings victorious,
We'll join in the chorus,
"The Lord will provide." (17)

No. 17.   JESUS THEN I KNOW.

C. S. R.   THEODORE E. PERKINS.

1. When my soul within Sorrowed with its sin, Je-sus swept the shades a-
2. And when oft oppressed, Wand'ring from my rest, Who was quick to see my

way; Christ, the Lord di-vine, Gave his life for mine,
grief? Je-sus, from a-bove, Shed his help-ful love,
D. S. *His the joys un-told, His the streets of gold,—*

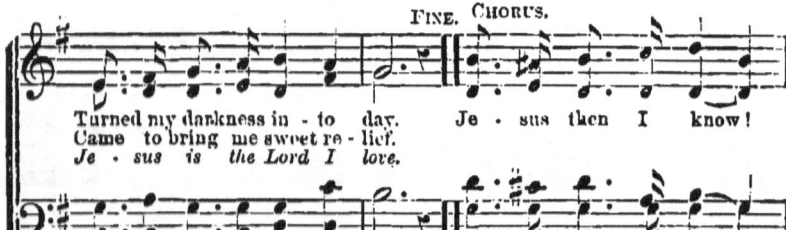

Turned my darkness in-to day.   Je-sus then I know!
Came to bring me sweet re-lief.
Je-sus is the Lord I love.

His the name be-low,— His the name to sing a-bove.

3 Now when every task
  Tries the faith I ask,
Who beside me comes to stand?
  Jesus, blessed Lord,
  Speaks the cheering word,
Takes me by the trembling hand. *Cho.*

4 And when failing breath
  Tells the hour of death,
Who will be my spirit's stay?
  Jesus, then will be
  Near to welcome me,
At the shining gates of day! *Cho.*

From " Calvary Songs," by per.

No. 18. ONWARD, CHRISTIAN SOLDIERS.

Rev. S. B. Gould.
Joseph Haydn, arr.

1. Onward, Christian soldiers, Marching as to war, With the Cross of Jesus
2. Like a mighty army Moves the Church of God; Brothers, we are treading

Going on before. Christ the Royal Master Leads against the foe,
Where the saints have trod; We are not divided, All one body we;

CHORUS.

Forward into battle, See, his banners go. Onward, Christian soldiers,
One in hope and doctrine, One in charity.

Marching as to war, With the Cross of Jesus Going on before.

3 Crowns and thrones may perish,
  Kingdoms rise and wane,
But the Church of Jesus
  Constant will remain;
Gates of hell can never
  'Gainst that Church prevail;
We have Christ's own promise,
  And that cannot fail.

4 Onward, then, ye people,
  Join our happy throng,
Blend with ours your voices
  In the triumph song;
Glory, laud, and honor,
  Unto Christ the King,
This thro' countless ages
  Men and angels sing.

No. 20. ALL TO CHRIST I OWE.

Mrs. Elvina M. Hall. John T. Grape, by per.

1. I hear the Sav-iour say, Thy strength in-deed is small;
Child of weakness, watch and pray, Find in Me thine all in all.

CHORUS.

Je-sus paid it all, All to Him I owe;
Sin had left a crimson stain: He washed it white as snow.

2 Lord, now indeed I find
  Thy power, and Thine alone,
Can change the leper's spot,
  And melt the heart of stone.

3 For nothing good have I
  Whereby Thy grace to claim—
I'll wash my garment white
  In the blood of Calvary's Lamb.

4 When from my dying bed
  My ransomed soul shall rise,
Then "Jesus paid it all"
  Shall rend the vaulted skies.

5 And when before the throne
  I stand in Him complete,
I'll lay my trophies down,
  All down at Jesus' feet.

No. 21. I'M KNEELING AT THE DOOR.

Mrs. LYDIA C. BAXTER. THEODORE E. PERKINS.

1. I'm kneel-ing, Lord, at mer- cy's gate, With trembling hope and fear, I've wait-ed long and still I wait Thy gracious voice to hear. Thy precious word has bid me seek The joys thou hast in store; Wilt thou, O Lord, in mer-cy speak, I'm kneeling at the door. I'm kneel-ing at the door, Kneel-ing at the door, Wilt thou, O Lord, in mer- cy speak, I'm kneeling at the door.

2. None ever empty turned away,
Who truly sought thy face:
And I, my Saviour, come to-day,
To seek thy pardoning grace.

I'M KNEELING AT THE DOOR.—CONCLUDED.

Thy precious blood is all my plea:
This, can my soul restore;
Wilt thou in mercy speak to me,
I'm kneeling at the door.

3 And when the ransomed millions stand
On Zion's flowery hill,
With palms of victory in their hand,
Waiting their Master's will:
Oh, may I bear the living green,
And that dear name adore,
Whose love the sinner did redeem,
While kneeling at the door.

No. 92.
FANNY CROSBY.

JESUS, MY ALL.

Arranged by
THEODORE E. PERKINS.

1. Lord, at thy mer-cy-seat, Humbly I fall;
Pleading thy prom-ise sweet, Lord, hear my call;
Now let thy work be-gin, Oh, make me pure with-in,
Cleanse me from ev-ery sin, Je-sus, my all.

2. Tears of repentant grief
Silently fall;
Help thou my unbelief,
Hear thou my call.
Oh, how I pine for thee!
'Tis all my hope, my plea:
Jesus has died for me;
Jesus, my all.

3. Hark! how the words of love
Tenderly fall,
Ere to the realms above,
Heard is my call;
Now every doubt has flown,
Broken my heart of stone,
Lord, I am thine alone,
Jesus, my all.

4. Still at thy mercy-seat
Humbly I fall;
Pleading thy promise sweet,
Heard is my call.
Faith wings my soul to thee,
This all my hope shall be,
Jesus has died for me,
Jesus, my all.

No. 23. WONDROUS LOVE.

Mrs. M. Stockton.   Wm. G. Fischer, by per.

1. God loved the world of sinners lost, And ruined by the fall;
Sal-vation full, at high-est cost, He of-fers free to all.

CHORUS.
Oh, 'twas love, 'twas wondrous love! The love of God to me: It brought my Sav-iour from a-bove, To die on Cal-va-ry.

2 Ev'n now by faith I claim him mine,
   The risen Son of God;
Redemption by his death I find,
   And cleansing thro' the blood.

3 Love brings the glorious fullness in,
   And to his saints makes known
The blessed rest from inbred sin,
   Thro' faith in Christ alone.

4 Believing souls, rejoicing go;
   There shall to you be given
A glorious foretaste, here below,
   Of endless life in heaven.

5 Of victory now o'er Satan's power
   Let all the ransomed sing,
And triumph in the dying hour
   Thro' Christ the Lord our King.

3 How the angel-band rejoices
  When a kneeling mortal prays;
  Hear them cry, in heavenly voices,
  "Keep on praying" all your days.
  Pray until you reach fair Canaan,
  Reach the pearly gates of day,
  Then your bliss shall end in glory,
  And shall never pass away.—Cho.

No. 25.   JESUS IS HERE.
Re-written by C. F. D.   PHILIP PHILLIPS, by per.

1. O, come to Jesus now, Jesus is here, Jesus is here;
2. O, come this place with-in, Jesus is here, Jesus is here;

All low before Him bow, Jesus is here, Jesus is here;
He sees you, full of sin, Jesus is here, Jesus is here;

Too many go a-way, Too many still de-lay, Tho'
He knows your heart of stone, He hears your spir-it groan, He

Jesus bids them stay; Jesus is here, Jesus is here.
heeds your pleading tone; Jesus is here, Jesus is here.

2 Come, then, to Jesus now,
   Jesus is here, Jesus is here;
All near him lowly bow,
   Jesus is here, Jesus is here,
O, ye that feel your sin,
And coming long have been,
Through faith your pardon win:
   Jesus is here, Jesus is here.

4 O, come to Jesus now,
   Jesus is here, Jesus is here;
Fathers and children bow,
   Jesus is here, Jesus is here.
O, what a glorious thing,
Sin's weary load to bring,
And lose it while we sing:
   Jesus is here, Jesus is here.

No. 26. LOOKING UNTO JESUS.

FANNY CROSBY.   THEODORE E. PERKINS.

1. Wea-ry not, my bro-ther, Cheer-ful be thy song; Is thy bur-den heav-y, And the jour-ney long? Does the weight op-press thee? Cast it on the Lord: Run thy race with pa-tience,
2. Seek and thou shalt find him, Still in faith be-lieve, Call and he will hear thee, Ask him, and re-ceive: In the dark-est mo-ment— In the deep-est night, He will give thee com-fort,

CHORUS.

Trusting in His word. Looking un-to Je-sus, He has died for thee. Oh, glo-ry be to Je-sus, We'll shout sal-va-tion's free.
He will give thee light.

3 Trials may befall thee,
   Thorns beset thy way,
Never mind them, brother,
   Only watch and pray:
Through the vale of sorrow
   Once the Saviour trod;
Run thy race with patience,
   Pressing on to God.

4 Labor on, my brother,
   Thou shalt reap at last
Fruits of joy eternal,
   When thy work is past;
Crowds of shining angels
   View thee from the skies,
Run thy race with patience,
   Yonder is the prize.

No. 27. THE GATE AJAR FOR ME.

Mrs. Lydia Baxter.   S. J. Vail, by per. Philip Phillips.

1. There is a gate that stands a-jar, And, thro' its por-tals gleaming,
2. That gate a-jar stands free to all Who seek thro' it sal-va-tion;

A radiance from the Cross a-far The Saviour's love re-veal-ing.
The rich and poor, the great and small, Of eve-ry tribe and na-tion.

REFRAIN.

Oh, depth of mer-cy! can it be That gate was left a-jar for me?

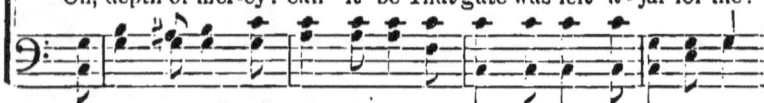

For me...... for me?.... Was left a-jar for me?

for me,   for me?

3 Press onward, then, tho' foes may frown,
While mercy's gate is open,
Accept the cross, and win the crown,
Love's everlasting token.

4 Beyond the river's brink we'll lay
The Cross that here is given,
And bear the Crown of life away,
And love Him more in heaven.

No. 29. HOME OF THE SOUL.

Mrs. Ellen H. Gates. From "Hallowed Songs," by per.

1. I will sing you a song of that beau-ti-ful land, The far a-way home of the soul, Where no storms ever beat on the glit-ter-ing strand, While the years of e-ter-ni-ty roll, While the years of e-ter-ni-ty roll; Where no storms ev-er

2. Oh, that home of the soul in my visions and dreams. Its bright jasper walls I can see; Till I fan-cy but thin-ly the vail in-ter-venes Be-tween that fair cit-y and me, Be-tween that fair cit-y and me; Till I fan-cy but

3. That un-chang-a-ble home is for you and for me, Where Je-sus of Naz-a-reth stands; The King of all kingdoms for-ev-er, is He, And He hold-eth our crown in His hands, And He hold-eth our crowns in His hands; The King of all

4. Oh, how sweet it will be in that beau-ti-ful land, So free from all sor-row and pain; With songs on our lips and with harps in our hands To meet one an-oth-er a-gain, To meet one an-oth-er a-gain; With songs on our

(30)

HOME OF THE SOUL.—CONCLUDED.

beat on that glit-ter-ing strand, While the years of e-ter-ni-ty roll.
thin-ly the vail in-ter-venes Be-tween the fair cit-y and me.
kingdoms for-ever is He, And He holdeth our crowns in His hands.
lips and with harps in our hands, To meet one an-oth-er a-gain.

No. 30. LEAD ME ON, KARL REDEN, by per.

1. Trav'ling to the better land, O'er the desert's scorching sand,
Fa-ther! let me grasp Thy hand; Lead me on, lead me on!

2.
When at Marah, parched with heat,
I the sparkling fountain greet,
Make the bitter waters sweet ;
    Lead me on !
3.
When the wilderness is drear,
Show me Elim's palm-groves near,
And her wells as crystal clear ;
    Lead me on !
4.
Through the water, thro' the fire,
Never let me fall or tire,
Every step brings Canaan nigher :
    Lead me on !

5.
Bid me stand on Nebo's height,
Gaze upon the land of light,
Then transported with the sight,
    Lead me on !
6.
When I stand on Jordan's brink,
Never let me fear or shrink ;
Hold me. Father, lest I sink ;
    Lead me on !
7.
When the victory is won,
And eternal life begun,
Up to glory lead me on !
    Lead me on, lead me on !

No. 31. BEYOND THE SMILING AND THE WEEPING.

Rev. H. Bonar, D.D.   Theodore E. Perkins.

1. Beyond the smiling and the weeping, I shall be soon; Beyond the waking and the sleeping, Beyond the sow-ing and the reap-ing, I shall be soon.
2. Beyond the blooming and the fad-ing, I shall be soon; Beyond the shining and the shading, Beyond the hop-ing and the dreading, I shall be soon.

CHORUS.

Love, rest and home! Sweet home, sweet home! Lord, tar-ry not, but come, Lord, tar-ry not, but come.

3 Beyond the parting and the meeting,
    I shall be soon;
  Beyond the farewell and the greeting,
  Beyond the pulse's fever beating,
    I shall be soon.—*Cho.*

4 Beyond the frost-chain and the fever,
    I shall be soon;
  Beyond the rock-waste and the river,
  Beyond the ever and the never,
    I shall be soon.—*Cho.*

No. 32.   IN THE PRESENCE OF THE KING.

Miss C. Armstrong.   English.

1. Oh, to be o-ver yon-der! In that land of wonder, Where the
2. Oh, to be o-ver yonder! My yearning heart grows fonder Of

an-gel voi-ces min-gle, and the angel harpers ring; To be
look-ing to the east, to see the blessed day-star bring Some

free from pain and sorrow, And the anxious dread to-morrow, To
tid-ings of the waking, The cloudless, pure day breaking, My

rest in light and sunshine in the presence of the King.
heart is yearning—yearning for the coming of the King.

3 Oh, to be over yonder!
   Alas! I sigh and wonder
Why clings my poor, weak, sinful
   heart to any earthly thing?
Each tie of earth must sever,
   And pass away forever,
But there's no more separation in
   the presence of the King.

4 Oh, when shall I be yonder?
   The longing groweth stronger
To join in all the praises the re-
   deemed ones do sing
Within those heavenly places,
   Where the angels vail their faces,
In awe and adoration in the pres-
   ence of the King.

No. 33. WHITER THAN SNOW.

JAMES NICHOLSON.   WM. G. FISCHER, by per.

1. Dear Jesus, I long to be per-fect-ly whole; I want Thee for-
2. Dear Jesus, come down from thy throne in the skies, And help me to

ev - er to live in my soul; Break down eve-ry i - dol, cast
make a complete sac-ri - fice; I give up my - self, and what-

out eve-ry foe; Now wash me, and I shall be whiter than snow.
ev - er I know: Now wash me, and I shall be whiter than snow.

CHORUS.

Whit-er than snow, yes, whit-er than snow; Now wash me, and
I shall be whiter than snow.

3.
Dear Jesus, for this I most humbly entreat;
I wait, blessed Lord, sitting low at Thy feet.
By faith, for my cleansing, I see the blood flow—
Now wash me, and I shall be, etc.

(34)

No. 34.   **NOTHING BUT LEAVES.**

Mrs. Lucy E. Akerman.   S. J. Vail, by per.

1. Nothing but leaves! The Spir-it grieves O'er years of wast-ed life; O'er sins in-dulged while conscience slept, O'er vows and prom-is-es un-kept, And reap from years of strife— Noth-ing but leaves! Noth-ing but leaves!

2. Nothing but leaves! No gather'd sheaves Of life's fair rip'-ning grain: We sow our seeds; lo! tares and weeds—Words, i-dle words, for ear-nest deeds —Then reap, with toil and pain, Noth-ing but leaves! Noth-ing but leaves!

3.
Nothing but leaves! Sad mem'ry weaves
No veil to hide the past:
And as we trace our weary way,
And count each lost and misspent day
We sadly find at last—
Nothing but leaves! nothing but leaves!

4.
Ah, who shall thus the Master meet,
And bring but withered leaves?
Ah, who shall at the Saviour's feet,
Before the awful judgment-seat
Lay down for golden sheaves,
Nothing but leaves! nothing but leaves!

CLING CLOSE TO THE ROCK.—CONCLUDED.

shock, Assured of sal-va-tion thro' Jesus the Rock.

No. 36. JESUS IS MINE.
BONAR. THEODORE E. PERKINS.

1. Fade, fade each earth-ly joy, Je-sus is mine! Break ev-ery ten-der tie, Je-sus is mine! Dark is the wil-derness, Earth has no rest-ing place, Je-sus a-lone can bless, Je-sus is mine!

Tempt not my soul away,
 Jesus is mine!
Here would I ever stay,
 Jesus is mine!
Perishing things of clay,
Born but for one brief day,
Pass from my heart away,
 Jesus is mine!

3 Farewell, ye dreams of night,
 Jesus is mine!
Lost in this dawning light,
 Jesus is mine!

All that my soul has tried,
Left but a dismal void,
Jesus has satisfied,
 Jesus is mine!

4 Farewell, mortality,
 Jesus is mine!
Welcome, eternity,
 Jesus is mine!
Welcome, O loved and blest,
Welcome, sweet scenes of rest,
Welcome, my Saviour's breast
 Jesus is mine!

No. 37. WE'LL WAIT TILL JESUS COMES.

DR. MILLER, by per.

1. O land of rest, for thee I sigh, When will the moment come,
When I shall lay my ar-mor by, And dwell in peace at home?

2. No tran-quil joys on earth I know, No peaceful shelt'ring dome,
This world's a wil-der-ness of woe, This world is not my home.

CHORUS.
We'll wait till Je-sus comes, We'll wait till Je-sus comes,
We'll wait till Je-sus comes, And we'll be gathered home.

3 To Jesus Christ I fled for rest;
He bade me cease to roam,
And lean for succor on His breast,
And He'd conduct me home.

4 I sought at once my Saviour's side,
No more my steps shall roam;
With Him I'll brave death's chilling [tide,
And reach my heav'nly home.

No. 40. COME, OH, COME WITH THY BROKEN HEART.
FANNY CROSBY.   THEODORE E. PERKINS.

2 Firmly cling to the blessed cross,
  There shall thy refuge be;
  Wash thee now in the crimson fount,
  Flowing so pure for thee:
  List to the gentle warning voice,
  List to the earnest call,
  Leave at the cross thy burden now,
  Jesus will bear it all.—*Cho.*

3 Come and taste of the precious Feast
  Of eternal love: [feast,
  Think of joys that forever bloom,
  Bright in the life above:
  Come with a trusting heart to God,
  Come and be saved by grace;
  Come, for He loves to clasp thee now,
  Close in His dear embrace. *Cho.*

No. 41. I SHALL NOT WANT.

Rev. Charles F. Deems. W. H. Monk, arr.

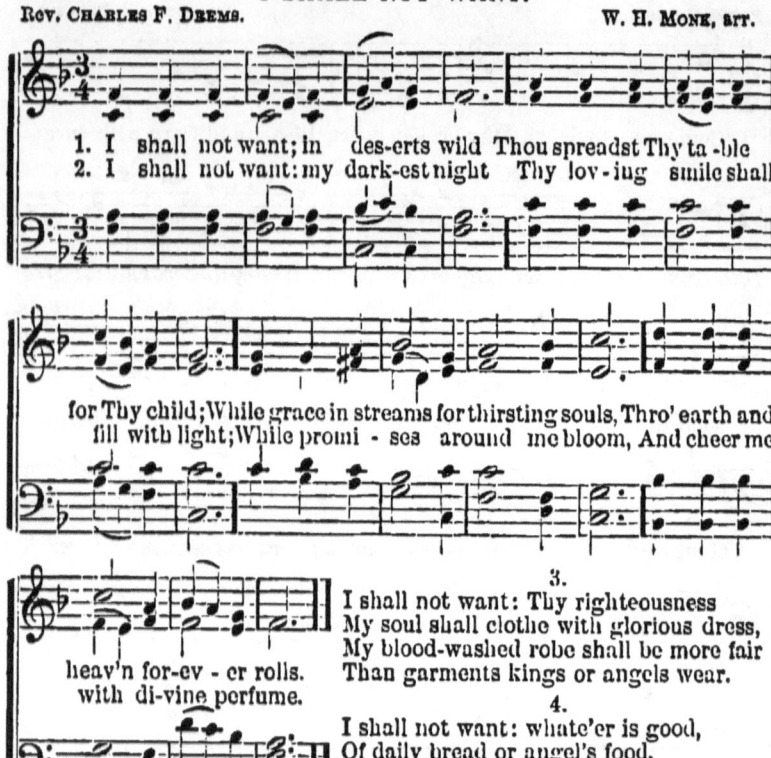

1. I shall not want; in des-erts wild Thou spreadst Thy ta-ble for Thy child; While grace in streams for thirsting souls, Thro' earth and heav'n for-ev-er rolls.

2. I shall not want: my dark-est night Thy lov-ing smile shall fill with light; While promi-ses around me bloom, And cheer me with di-vine perfume.

3.
I shall not want: Thy righteousness
My soul shall clothe with glorious dress,
My blood-washed robe shall be more fair
Than garments kings or angels wear.

4.
I shall not want: whate'er is good,
Of daily bread or angel's food,
Shall to my Father's child be sure,
So long as earth and heaven endure.

No. 42.

1.
Sun of my soul, Thou Saviour dear,
It is not night if Thou be near;
Oh, may no earth-born cloud arise,
To hide Thee from Thy servant's eyes.

2.
When the soft dews of kindly sleep
My wearied eye-lids gently steep,
Be my last thought, how sweet to rest
Forever on my Saviour's breast.

3.
Abide with me from morn till eve,
For without Thee I cannot live;
Abide with me when night is nigh,
For without Thee I dare not die.

4.
If some poor wand'ring child of Thine
Have spurned to-day the voice divine
Now, Lord, the gracious work begin;
Let him no more lie down in sin.

5.
Watch by the sick; enrich the poor
With blessings from Thy boundless store;
Be every mourner's sleep to-night,
Like infant's slumbers, pure and light.

6.
Come near and bless us when we wake,
Ere through the world our way we take,
Till in the ocean of Thy love
We lose ourselves in heaven above.

(42)

No. 43.   THINE FOREVER.
M. F. MAUDE.   THEODORE E. PERKINS.

1. Hear us from Thy throne above, Thine forever—ever—God of love!
Here and in e-ter-ni-ty, Thine forev-er—ever—may we be.

REFRAIN.
Show the way! Show the way! Guide us to the realms of day,
Show the way! Show the way! Guide us to the realms of day,
Shield us thro' the earthly strife, Thine forever—ever—Lord of life!

2 They who find in Thee their rest,
   Thine forever—ever-oh, how blest!
Oh, defend us to the end,
   Guardian Saviour, Saviour, heavenly Friend!

3 Let us all thy goodness share,
   Sheltered only—only—in Thy care,
These Thy frail and trembling sheep,
   Thine forever—ever—Saviour, keep.

No. 44. GATHERING HOME.

MARY LESLIE. W. A. OGDEN.

(44)

GATHERING HOME.—CONCLUDED.

riv-er one by one; Gath'ring home, gath'ring home, Yes, one by one.

2 We, too, shall come to the river side,
　　One by one, one by one;
　We are nearer its waters each eventide,
　　Yes, one by one;
　We can hear the noise and the dashing stream,
　Oft now and again thro' our life's deep dream;
　Sometimes the dark floods all the banks overflow,
　Sometimes in ripples and small waves go.

3 Jesus, Redeemer, we look to Thee,
　　One by one, one by one;
　We lift up our voices tremblingly,
　　Yes, one by one;
　The waves of the river are dark and cold,
　We know not the place where our feet may hold;
　O Thou who didst pass thro' in deepest midnight,
　Now guide us, send us the staff and light.

No. 45.　　　　TO-DAY. 6 & 4.
Rev. S. F. Smith.　　　　　　　　　Dr. L. Mason, 1831.

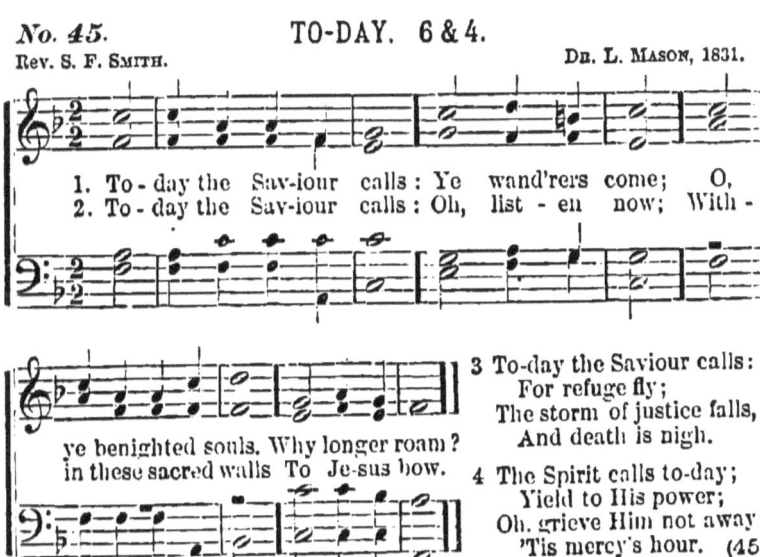

1. To-day the Saviour calls: Ye wand'rers come; O,
2. To-day the Saviour calls: Oh, listen now; With-

ye benighted souls. Why longer roam?
in these sacred walls To Jesus bow.

3 To-day the Saviour calls:
　For refuge fly;
　The storm of justice falls,
　And death is nigh.

4 The Spirit calls to-day;
　Yield to His power;
　Oh, grieve Him not away;
　'Tis mercy's hour.　(45)

Nearer in prayer my hope aspires,
I'm coming nearer;
Deeper the love my soul desires,
I'm coming nearer;
Nearer the end of toil and care,
Nearer the crown I soon shall wear,
I'm coming nearer.

No. 47. BATTLING FOR THE LORD.

THEODORE E. PERKINS.

SEMI-CHORUS. / CHORUS.

1. We've list - ed in a ho - ly war, Battling for the Lord!
2. We've gird - ed on our armor bright, Battling for the Lord!
3. We'll stand like he - roes on the field, Battling for the Lord!
4. Though sin and death our way oppose, Battling for the Lord!
5. And when our glorious war is o'er, Battling for the Lord!

SEMI-CHORUS. / CHORUS.

E - ter - nal life, our guiding star, Battling for the Lord!
Our Captain's word our strength and might, Battling for the Lord!
And no - bly fight but nev - er yield, Battling for the Lord!
Thro' grace we'll conquer all our foes, Battling for the Lord!
We'll shout sal - va - tion ev - er - more, Battling for the Lord!

FULL CHORUS.

We'll work till Je - sus comes, We'll work till Je - sus comes,

We'll work till Je - sus comes. And then we'll rest at home.

(47)

I LOVE TO TELL THE STORY.—CONCLUDED.

To tell the old, old sto-ry, Of Je-sus and His love.

3 I love to tell the story;
'Tis pleasant to repeat
What seems, each time I tell it,
More wonderfully sweet.
I love to tell the story;
For some have never heard
The message of salvation,
From God's own holy word.

4 I love to tell the story;
For those who know it best
Seem hungering and thirsting
To hear it like the rest.
And when, in scenes of glory,
I sing the New, New Song,
'Twill be the Old, Old Story
That I have loved so long!

No. 49.   ROCK OF AGES.

Rev. A. Toplady.   Dr. Thomas Hastings.

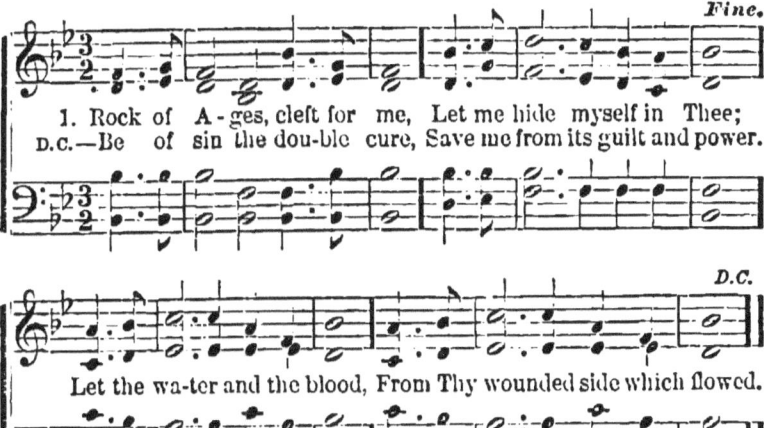

1. Rock of A-ges, cleft for me, Let me hide myself in Thee;
D.C.—Be of sin the dou-ble cure, Save me from its guilt and power.

Let the wa-ter and the blood, From Thy wounded side which flowed.

2 Not the labor of my hands
Can fulfil Thy law's demands;
Could my zeal no respite know,
Could my tears forever flow,
These for sin could not atone;
Thou must save, and Thou alone.

3 In my hand no price I bring,
Simply to Thy cross I cling;
Naked, come to Thee for dress,

Helpless, look to Thee for grace;
Foul, I to the fountain fly,
Wash me, Saviour, or I die.

4 While I draw this fleeting breath,
When mine eyes shall close in death,
When I soar to worlds unknown,
And behold Thee on Thy throne,—
Rock of Ages, cleft for me,
Let me hide myself in Thee.

JESUS OF NAZARETH PASSETH BY.—CONCLUDED.

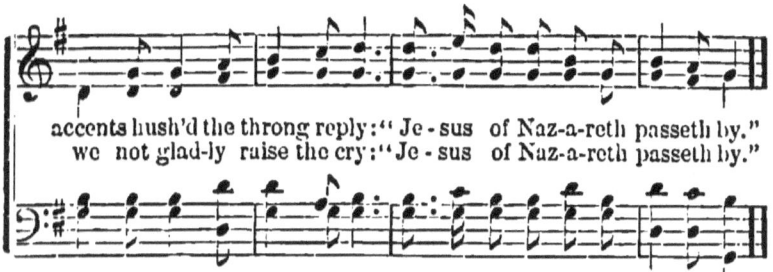

accents hush'd the throng reply: "Je-sus of Naz-a-reth passeth by."
we not glad-ly raise the cry: "Je-sus of Naz-a-reth passeth by."

3 Ho! all ye heavy-laden come!
Here's pardon, comfort, rest and home.
Ye wanderers from a Father's face,
Return, accept His proffered grace,
Ye tempted ones, there's refuge nigh:
"Jesus of Nazareth passeth by."

4 But, if you still this call refuse,
And all His wondrous love abuse,
Soon will He sadly from you turn,
Your bitter prayer for pardon spurn,
"Too late! too late!" will be the cry—
"Jesus of Nazareth *has passed by.*"

No. 51.   LABAN. S. M.
GEO. HEATH, 1781.   Dr. LOWELL MASON, 1830.

1. My soul, be on thy guard, Ten thousand foes a-rise;
2. O watch, and fight, and pray; The bat-tle ne'er give o'er;

The hosts of sin are pressing hard, To draw thee from the skies.
Re-new it bold-ly ev-ery day, And help di-vine implore.

3 Ne'er think the vict'ry won,
Nor lay thine armor down:
The work of faith will not be done,
Till thou obtain the crown.

4 Then persevere till death
Shall bring thee to thy God;
He'll take thee, at thy parting breath,
To His divine abode.

(51)

WHY NOT TELL JESUS ALL?—CONCLUDED.

Fall at His feet, confess to Him your sins, Why not tell Jesus all?

No. 53.   DENNIS. S. M.
REV. JOHN FAWCETT, 1772.   From H. G. NAGELI.

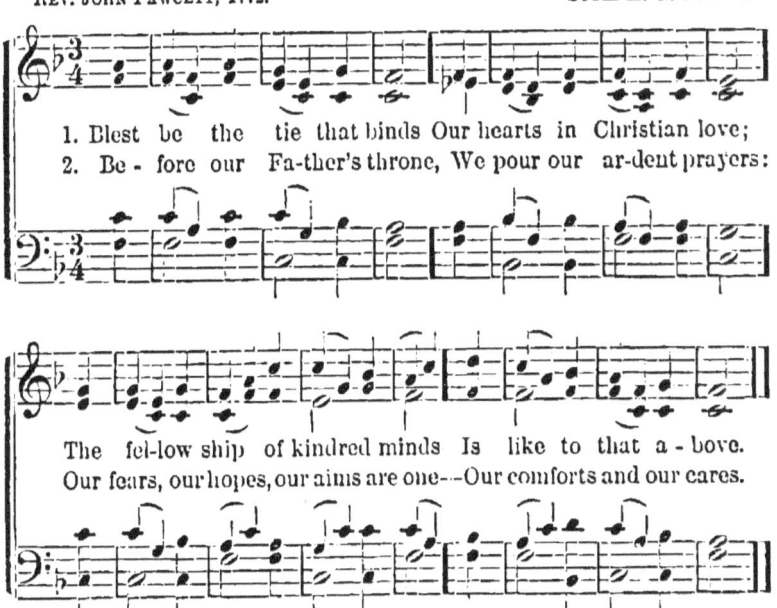

1. Blest be the tie that binds Our hearts in Christian love;
   The fel-low ship of kindred minds Is like to that a-bove.
2. Be-fore our Father's throne, We pour our ar-dent prayers:
   Our fears, our hopes, our aims are one—Our comforts and our cares.

3 We share our mutual woes:
   Our mutual burdens bear;
   And often for each other flows
   The sympathizing tear.

4 When we asunder part,
   It gives us inward pain;
   But we shall still be join'd in heart,
   And hope to meet again.

5 This glorious hope revives
   Our courage by the way;
   While each in expectation lives,
   And longs to see the day.

6 From sorrow, toil and pain,
   And sin, we shall be free,
   And perfect love and friendship
   Through all eternity.   [reign

THE ROCK THAT IS HIGHER.—CONCLUDED.

2.
Oh, sometimes how long seems the day,
 And sometimes how weary my feet;
But toiling in life's dusty way,
 The Rock's blessed shadow how sweet.

CHORUS.
Oh, then, to the Rock let me fly, let me fly
 To the Rock that is higher than I:
Oh, then to the Rock let me fly, let me fly,
 To the Rock that is higher than I.

3.
Oh, near to the Rock let me keep,
 If blessings, or sorrows prevail;
Or climbing the mountain way steep,
 Or walking the shadowy vale.

CHORUS.
Then, quick to the Rock I can fly, I can fly
 To the Rock that is higher than I:
Then, quick to the Rock I can fly, I can fly
 To the Rock that is higher than I.

No. 55.   JESUS, LOVER OF MY SOUL.

CHARLES WESLEY.   S. B. MARSH.

2.
Other refuge have I none,
 Hangs my helpless soul on Thee;
Leave, oh, leave me not alone,
 Still support and comfort me.
All my trust on Thee is stayed
 All my help from Thee I bring;
Cover my defenceless head
 With the shadow of Thy wing.

3.
Thou, O Christ, art all I want,
 More than all in Thee I find:
Raise the fallen, cheer the faint,
 Heal the sick, and lead the blind.

Just and holy is Thy Name,
 I am all unrighteousness:
Vile, and full of sin I am,
 Thou art full of truth and grace.

4.
Plenteous grace with Thee is found,
 Grace to cover all my sin :
Let the healing streams abound;
 Make me, keep me, pure within.
Thou of life the Fountain art,
 Freely let me take of Thee;
Spring Thou up within my heart,
 Rise to all eternity.

No. 56. JESUS, I AM WAITING NOW.

ELLA CHEEK. J. H. ANDERSON, by per.

1. Je-sus, I am wait-ing now, Wea-ry, worn, and weak;
Ah! the cross, I'm bend-ing low, Peace and rest I seek.

CHORUS.

Je-sus, I am wait-ing now, Long-ing to be blest;
Speak the bless-ed word to me, "Come, I'll give you rest."

2 Long I've wandered far from Thee,
   In the path of sin;
   Let my sorrow plead for me;
   Jesus, take me in.—*Cho.*

3 Chase my heart's unrest away,
   Bid its troubling cease;
   Let me feel thy love to-day;
   Give me Thy sweet peace.—*Cho.*

No. 58. SCATTER SEEDS OF KINDNESS.

Mrs. E. H. Gates. S. J. Vail. Cop. 1870.

1. Let us gath-er up the sunbeams Lying all around our path;
2. Strange, we never prize the music Till the sweet-voiced bird has flown!
3. If we knew the ba - by fingers, Press'd against the window pane,
4. Ah! those little ice-cold fingers, How they point our mem'ries back

Let us keep the wheat and roses, Casting out the thorns and chaff;
Strange, that we should slight the violets, Till the love-ly flow'rs are gone!
Would be cold and stiff to-morrow—Never trou-ble us a-gain—
To the has-ty words and actions Strewn along our backward track!

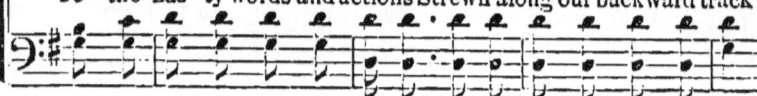

Let us find our sweetest comfort In the blessings of to-day,
Strange, that summer skies and sunshine Never seem one half so fair,
Would the bright eyes of our darl-ing Catch the frown up-on our brow!
How those lit-tle hands remind us, As in snow-y grace they lie,

With a pa-tient hand re-mov-ing All the bri-ars from the way.
As when winter's snow-y pinions Shake the white down in the air.
Would the print of ro-sy fingers Vex us then as they do now?
Not to scatter thorns—but ro-ses—For our reap-ing by and by.

SCATTER SEEDS OF KINDNESS.—CONCLUDED.

CHORUS.

Then scatter seeds of kindness, Then scat-ter seeds of kindness,

Then scatter seeds of kindness, For our reaping by-and-by.

No. 59.   CROSS AND CROWN.
G. N. ALLEN.   A. CHAPIN.

1. Must Jesus bear the cross a-lone, And all the world go free?
No, there's a cross for every one, And there's a cross for me.

2 How happy are the saints above,
  Who once went sorrowing here;
  But now they taste unmingled love,
  And joy without a tear.

3 The consecrated cross I'll bear,
  Till death shall set me free;
  And then go home my crown to wear,
  For there's a crown for me!

THE HOME OVER THERE.—CONCLUDED.

O-ver there, o-ver there, Oh, think of the home o-ver there.
O-ver there, o-ver there, Oh, think of the friends over there.

3.
My Saviour is now over there,
There my kindred and friends are at rest;
Then away from my sorrow and care,
Let me fly to the land of the blest.
Over there, over there,
My Saviour is now over there.

4.
I'll soon be at home over there,
For the end of my journey I see;
Many dear to my heart, over there,
Are watching and waiting for me.
Over there, over there,
I'll soon be at home over there.

No. 61.   ARLINGTON. C. M.
Rev. ISAAC WATTS.   THOS. A. ARNE.

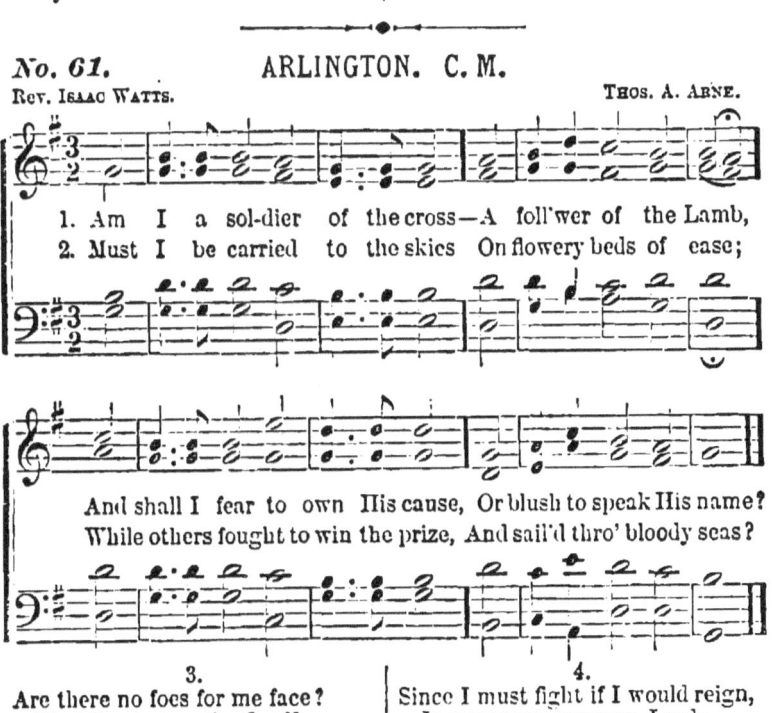

1. Am I a sol-dier of the cross—A foll'wer of the Lamb,
2. Must I be carried to the skies On flowery beds of ease;

And shall I fear to own His cause, Or blush to speak His name?
While others fought to win the prize, And sail'd thro' bloody seas?

3.
Are there no foes for me face?
Must I not stem the flood?
Is this vile world a friend to grace,
To help me on to God?

4.
Since I must fight if I would reign,
Increase my courage, Lord;
I'll bear the toil, endure the pain,
Supported by Thy word.

(61)

No. 62. **REST, PILGRIM, REST.**

Words arranged and Music by THEODORE E. PERKINS.

3 Rest in the shadow of the Rock, O pilgrim,
　　Rest, pilgrim, rest;
They who slumber by the Rock so dear,
Wake rejoicing, for their home is near,
　　Beneath its shade
　　Thy bed is made:
Rest in the shadow of the Rock, O Pilgrim,
　　Rest, pilgrim, rest.

No. 63. SAFE WITHIN THE VAIL.

Rev. E. Adams.   J. M. Evans, by per.

1. "Land a-head!" its fruits are wav-ing O'er the hills of fade-less green; And the liv-ing waters laving Shores where heav'nly forms are seen.
2. On-ward, bark! the cape I'm rounding; See the bless-ed wave their hands; Hear the harps of God resounding From the bright immortal bands.
3. There, "let go the an-chor," rid-ing On this calm and silv-'ry bay; Sea-ward fast the tide is gliding, Shores in sun-light stretch away.
4. Now we're safe from all tempt-a-tion, All the storms of life are past; Praise the Rock of our sal-va-tion, We are safe at home at last.

CHORUS.

Rocks and storms I'll fear no more, When on that e-ter-nal shore; Drop the an-chor! Furl the sail! I am safe with-in the vail!

BRIGHTLY GLEAMS.—CONCLUDED.

Pointing to the sky, Waving wand'rers onward To their homes on high.

No. 65.   NETTLETON.   8s & 7s.

Rev. R. Robinson.   Old Melody.

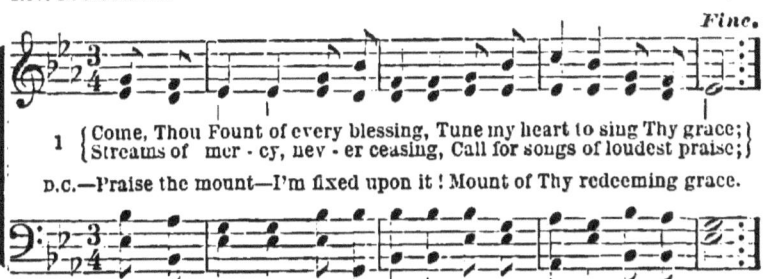

1 { Come, Thou Fount of every blessing, Tune my heart to sing Thy grace;
    Streams of mer - cy, nev - er ceasing, Call for songs of loudest praise; }

D.C.—Praise the mount—I'm fixed upon it! Mount of Thy redeeming grace.

Teach me some me-lo-dious son-net, Sung by flaming tongues above;

2.
Here I'll raise my Ebenezer,
 Hither by Thy help I'm come;
And I hope by Thy good pleasure,
 Safely to arrive at home.
Jesus sought me when a stranger,
 Wand'ring from the fold of God;
He to rescue me from danger,
 Interposed His precious blood.

3.
Oh, to grace how great a debtor,
 Daily I'm constrained to be!
Let Thy goodness like a fetter,
 Bind my wand'ring heart to Thee;
Prone to wander, Lord, I feel it—
 Prone to leave the God I love—
Here's my heart, O take and seal it,
 Seal it for Thy courts above.

No. 66. ON THE CROSS.

Words and Music by W. A. Ogden, by per.

1. The bless-ed Sav-iour died for me, On the cross, on the cross;
He bore my sins at Cal-va-ry, On the rug-ged cross.
Be-hold His hands and feet and side, The crown of thorns, the crimson tide, "Forgive them, Father," loud He cried, On the rugged cross.

2.
He now is calling unto me
　In His word, in His word;
He bids me drink life's waters free,
　In His blessed word.
For me His life He freely gave,
My guilty soul from sin to save;
His precious promises I have
　In His blessed word.

(66)

3.
O Saviour, touch my heart of sin,
　With Thy love, with Thy love;
And let the light of glory in,
　With Thy precious love.
Then I will join to praise Thy name,
To spread abroad Thy wondrous fame,
And all Thy promises will claim,
　With Thy precious love.

No. 67. ONLY TRUST HIM.

Rev. J. H. S. Rev. J. H. Stockton, by per.

1. Come, eve-ry soul by sin oppress'd. There's mer-cy with the Lord,
2. For Je-sus shed His precious blood Rich blessings to bestow;

And He will sure-ly give you rest, By trust-ing in His word.
Plunge now in-to the crimson flood That washes white as snow.

CHORUS.

On-ly trust Him, on-ly trust Him, On-ly trust Him now;

He will save you, He will save you, He will save you now.

3.
Yes, Jesus is the Truth, the way,
That leads you into rest:
Believe in Him without delay,
And you are fully blest.

4.
Come then, and join this holy band,
And on to glory go,
To dwell in that celestial land,
Where joys immortal flow.

No. 68.   **I AM PRAYING FOR YOU.**

S. O'MALEY CLUFF.   IRA D. SANKEY, by per.

1. I have a Saviour, He's pleading in glo-ry, A dear, loving Saviour tho' earth-friends be few; And now He is watching in tenderness o'er me, And oh that my Saviour were your Saviour too!
2. I have a Father: to me He has giv-en A hope for eter-ni-ty, bless-ed and true; And soon will He call me to meet Him in heav-en, But oh that He'd let me bring you with me too!
3. I have a robe: 'tis re-splendent in whiteness, A-waiting in glo-ry my won-der-ing view; Oh, when I re-ceive it all shin-ing in brightness, Dear friend, could I see you re-ceiv-ing one too!

CHORUS.

For you I am pray-ing, For you I am

I AM PRAYING FOR YOU.—CONCLUDED.

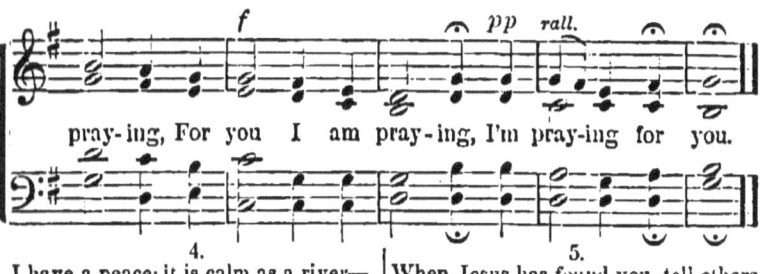

4.
I have a peace: it is calm as a river—
A peace that the friends of this world never knew;
My Saviour alone is its Author and Giver,
And oh, could I know it was give to you!

5.
When Jesus has found you, tell others the story,
That my loving Saviour is your Saviour too;
Then pray that your Saviour may bring them to glory,
And prayer will be answered—'twas answered for you!

No. 69. BOYLSTON. S. M.
Rev. Isaac Watts.   Dr. L. Mason.

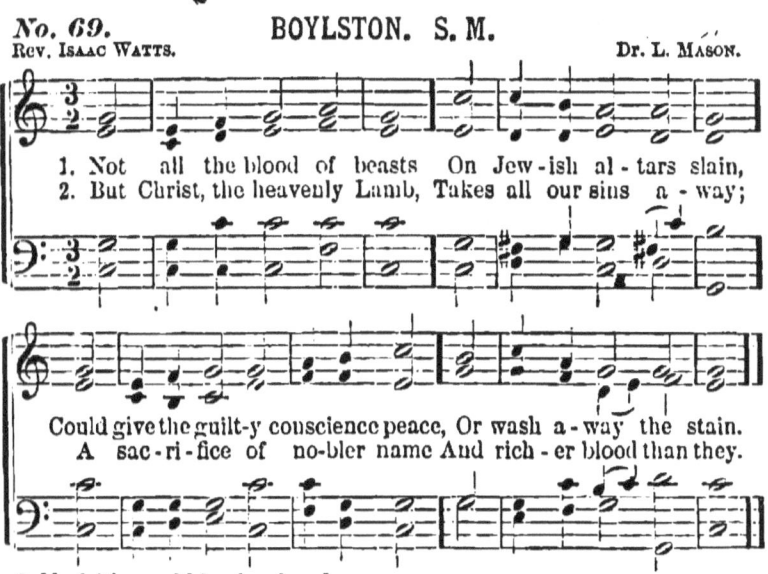

1. Not all the blood of beasts On Jewish altars slain,
Could give the guilty conscience peace, Or wash away the stain.
2. But Christ, the heavenly Lamb, Takes all our sins away;
A sacrifice of nobler name And richer blood than they.

3 My faith would lay her hand
On that dear head of thine,
While like a penitent I stand,
And there confess my sin.

4 My soul looks back to see
The burden thou did'st bear,
While hanging on the cursed tree,
And knows her guilt was there.

No. 70.
1 Did Christ o'er sinners weep,
And shall our cheeks be dry?
Let floods of penitential grief
Burst forth from every eye.

2 The Son of God in tears
The wond'ring angels see;
Be thou astonish'd, O my soul;
He shed those tears for thee.

3 He wept that we might weep;
Each sin demands a tear:
In heaven alone no sin is found,
And there's no weeping there.

No. 71. O, YE THAT ARE WEARY.

Rev. F. Bottome, D.D.   Sir Henry R. Bishop.

1. O, ye that are wea-ry and la-den of soul, Come, come to the fountain that maketh you whole; There's peace in believing, there's rest in His name, There's healing for all in the blood of the Lamb.

2. O cease from your anguish ye toil-ers for life, For vain is your la-bor and fruitless your strife, No hope can they bring you, no joy to your heart, None, none but the Saviour can resting impart.

CHORUS.

Rest, rest, sweet, sweet rest, In the bosom of Jesus there on-ly is rest.

3 Then come to the Saviour, ye weary and worn,
Your burdens and sorrows for you He hath borne;
No anguish that pierced but pierced Him before,
No thorn is so sharp as the crown which He wore.—*Cho.*

4 Rest, rest, blessed Jesus, O sweet rest at last,
Like calm on the ocean when tempest is past;
The morning-light breaketh in joy from above,
And illumines my soul with His rainbow of love.—*Cho.*

No. 72.   I AM WAITING BY THE RIVER.

WM. O. CUSHING.   Dr. THOS. HASTINGS.

1. I am wait-ing by the riv-er, And my heart has wait-ed long;
Now I think I hear the cho-rus Of the an-gel's welcome song,
Oh, I see the dawn is breaking On the hill-tops of the blest,
"Where the wick-ed cease from troubling, And the weary be at rest."

2.
Far away beyond the shadows
Of this weary vale of tears,
There the tide of bliss is sweeping
Thro' the bright and changeless years;
O! I long to be with Jesus,
In the mansions of the blest,
"Where the wicked cease from troubling,
And the weary be at rest."

3.
They are launching on the river,
From the calm and quiet shore,
And they soon will bear my spirit
Where the weary sigh no more:
For the tide is swiftly flowing,
And I long to greet the blest,
"Where the wicked cease from troubling,
And the weary be at rest."

No. 73. SAVIOUR! I FOLLOW ON.
CHARLES S. ROBINSON, D.D.　　　　　KARL REDEN, by per.

1. Saviour! I follow on, Guided by thee, Seeing not yet the hand That leadeth me; Hushed be my heart and still, Fear I no further ill, Only to meet Thy will My will shall be.

2 Riven the rock for me
　Thirst to relieve,,
　Manna from heaven falls
　Fresh every eve;
‖: Never a want severe
　Causeth my eye a tear,
　But thou dost whisper near,
　"Only believe!" :‖

3 Often to Marah's brink
　Have I been brought:
　Shrinking the cup to drink,
　Help I have sought;
‖: And with the prayer's ascent,
　Jesus the branch hath rent,
　Quickly relief hath sent,
　Sweetening the draught. :‖

4 Saviour! I long to walk
　Closer with thee;
　Led by thy guiding hand,
　Ever to be;
‖: Constantly near thy side,
　Quickened and purified,
　Living for him who died
　Freely for me! :‖

AROUND THE CROSS.

Words and Music by ROBERT EDWARDS.

1. An o-pen fountain rich and clear Around the cross I see,
2. Be-hold! behold! the bleeding Lamb, He comes to you once more;
3. He speaks in love's sweet kindly tone, To ease your troubled breast.

Where sinners go, and quench their thirst, And lo! the draught is free.
Oh! do not bid him go a-way, As you have done be-fore.
Ye! wea-ry souls, come un-to me, And I *will* give you rest.

CHORUS.

"Around the cross, around the cross, Sal-va-tion's gift is free.

By Je-sus purchased with his blood That flowed for "*you* and *me.*"

4.
Why treat so ill your dearest friend
Who bled and died for you?
He pleads your cause before the throne
As none but He could do.—CHO.

5.
Raised by the cross around the throne,
When life's short day is o'er,
Our souls the glories of the cross,
Shall praise forever more.

Copyright, 1878, by Robert Edwards.

No. 76. WHY, SINNER, WHY?

JOSEPHINE POLLARD.   *From "Crystal Songs," by per.*   LUCY J. RIDER.

1. Why wilt thou not re-lent? Why, sin-ner, why?
2. Dost thou not hear His voice, Come, sin-ner, come?
3. Un-to the mer-cy-seat, Fly, sin-ner, fly;

Why wilt thou not re-pent? Why, sin-ner, why?
Bid-ing thee make thy choice, Come, sin-ner, come:
Un-to the Sav-iour's feet, Fly, sin-ner, fly:

Je-sus draws near to-day, His mer-cy to display;
He will es-cape af-ford, From the de-stroy-er's sword;
This is thy day of grace, Je-sus un-veils His face:

Why wilt thou turn a-way? Why, sin-ner, why?
Un-to thy wait-ing Lord Come, sin-ner, come.
Un-to His glad embrace Fly, sin-ner, fly.

(75)

No. 77. MY FAITH LOOKS UP TO THEE.

Rev. Ray Palmer, D. D.   Dr. Thos. Hastings.

1. My faith looks up to Thee, Thou Lamb of Calvary; Saviour divine; Now hear me while I pray; Take all my guilt away; O, let me, from this day, Be wholly Thine.

2 May Thy rich grace impart
  Strength to my fainting heart:
    My zeal inspire;
  As Thou hast died for me,
  O may my love to Thee
  Pure, warm, and changeless be—
    A living fire.

3 While life's dark maze I tread,
  And griefs around me spread,
    Be Thou my guide:
  Bid darkness turn to day;
  Wipe sorrow's tears away.
  Nor let me ever stray
    From Thee aside.

4 When ends life's transient dream:
  When death's cold sullen stream
    Shall o'er me roll;
  Blest Saviour, then in love,
  Fear and distress remove;
  O bear me safe above,—
    A ransom'd soul.

No. 78.   Tune—*Bethany.*

1 Nearer, my God, to thee.
    Nearer to thee!
  Ev'n though it be a cross
    That raiseth me,
  Still all my song shall be,
  Nearer, my God, to thee,
    Nearer to thee!

2 Though like a wanderer,
    The sun gone down,
  Darkness comes over me,
    My rest a stone,
  Yet in my dreams I'd be
  Nearer, my God, to thee,
    Nearer to thee!

3 There let my way appear
    Steps unto heaven;
  All that thou sendest me
    In mercy given;
  Angels to beckon me
  Nearer, my God, to thee,
    Nearer to thee!

No. 79. ARISE, MY SOUL, ARISE.
Rev. Charles Wesley. J. Edson.

1. A-rise, my soul, a-rise, Shake off thy guilt-y fears The bleeding sac-ri-fice In my be-half ap-pears; Be-fore the throne my Sure-ty stands, My name is writ-ten on His hands, My name is writ-ten on His hands.

2 He ever lives above,
   For me to intercede,
His all redeeming love,
   His precious blood to plead;
His blood atoned for all our race,
And sprinkles now the throne of grace.

3 Five bleeding wounds He bears,
   Received on Calvary:
They pour effectual prayers,
   They strongly plead for me:
Forgive him, oh, forgive, they cry,
Nor let that ransomed sinner die.

4 The Father hears him pray,
   His dear anointed One:
He cannot turn away
   The presence of his Son:
His Spirit answers to the blood,
And tells me I am born of God.

5 My God is reconciled;
   His pardoning voice I hear;
He owns me for His child;
   I can no longer fear;
With confidence I now draw nigh,
And Father, Abba, Father cry.

JESUS WILL WELCOME ME.—CONCLUDED.

Onward, Jesus will welcome me home.
cheering me onward,

No. 81. I CLING TO THEE.
C. ELLIOTT. FLEMMING.

1. O Holy Saviour! Friend unseen, Since on thine arm thou bid'st me lean, Help me throughout life's changing scene, By faith to cling to Thee.
2. What tho' the world deceitful prove, And earthly friends and hopes remove; With patient, uncomplaining love, Still would I cling to Thee.

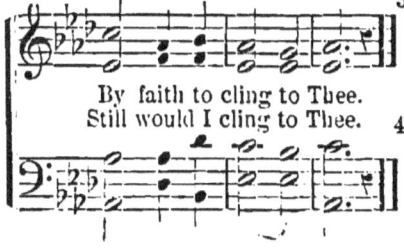

3 Though oft I seem to tread alone
  Life's dreary waste, with thorns o'er-grown,
  Thy voice of love, in gentlest tone,
  Still whispers, "Cling to me!"
4 Though faith and hope are often tried,
  I ask not, need not, aught beside;
  So safe, so calm, so satisfied,
  The soul that clings to Thee!

No. 82. GIVE YOURSELF TO JESUS, WHOLLY.

KARL REDEN, by per.

1. Give yourself to Jesus, whol-ly, He has bought you with His blood: He de-sir-eth your sal-va-tion; He would bring you home to God: Small re-turn for love so ten-der, Small re-turn for love so true, Is your heart with all its
2. Give yourself to Jesus, whol-ly, His to be e-ter-nal-ly; Where and what your Lord would have you Ev - er wil-ling just to be: Fol-low close-ly where He lead-eth,— It will be in pastures sweet; Hap-py if for Je-sus
3. Give yourself to Jesus, whol-ly, On His bosom lean and rest; In His love se-cure a-bid-ing; In that love complete-ly blest: All your hearts to Him up-lift-ed, All your will in His con-trol; Be your life one glad com-

GIVE YOURSELF TO JESUS, WHOLLY.—CONCLUDED.

weak - ness, Yet, 'tis all He asks of you.
toil - ing; Hap - py, wait - ing at His feet.
mun - ion With the Sav - iour of your soul.

No. 83. THERE IS A LAND.

Rev. Dr. Watts.   Geo. F. Root, by per.

1. { There is a land of pure delight, Where saints immortal reign;
E - ter - nal day excludes the night, And pleasures banish pain. }

There ev - er-last-ing spring abides, And nev - er with'ring flowers;

Death, like a nar-row sea divides This heavenly land of ours.

2 Sweet fields beyond the swelling flood
Stand dressed in living green;
So to the Jews old Canaan stood,
While Jordan rolled between:

3 Could we but climb where Moses stood,
And view the landscape o'er,
No Jordan stream of death's cold flood,
Should fright us from the shore.

(81)

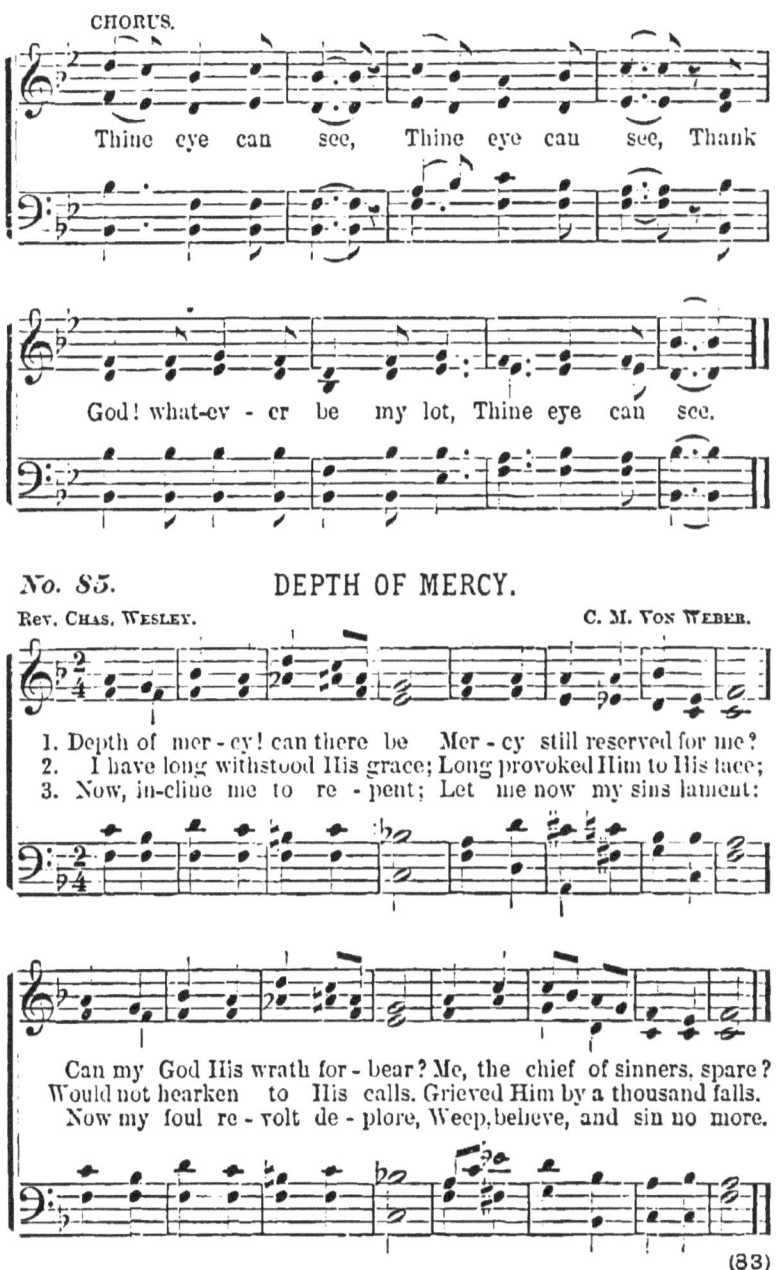

No. 86.   NOT NOW, MY CHILD.
Mrs. Catherine Penefather, 1863.   Ira D. Sankey, by per.
Slow, and with expression.

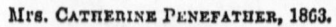

1. Not now, my child—a lit-tle more rough tossing, A
2. Not now; for I have wanderers in the distance, And

lit-tle long-er on the bil-low's foam; A few more journeyings
thou must call them in with patient love; Not now, for I have

in the desert darkness, And then, the sunshine of thy Father's Home!
sheep upon the mountains, And thou must follow them where'er they rove.

3 Not now, for I have loved ones sad and weary;
  Wilt thou not cheer them with a kindly smile?
  Sick ones, who need thee in their lonely sorrow;
  Wilt thou not tend them yet a little while?

4 Not now; for wounded hearts are sorely bleeding,
  And thou must teach those widowed hearts to sing:
  Not now; for orphans' tears are quickly falling,
  They must be gathered 'neath some sheltering wing.

5 Go, with the name of Jesus, to the dying,
  And speak that Name in all its living power;
  Why should thy fainting heart grow chill and weary?
  Canst thou not watch with Me one little hour?

6 One little hour! and then the glorious crowning,
  The golden harp-strings, and the victor's palm;
  One little hour! and then the hallelujah!
  Eternity's long, deep, thanksgiving psalm!

(84)

HORTON. 7s.

87.

1 Come, my soul, thy suit prepare,
Jesus loves to answer prayer:
He himself hath bid thee pray,
Rise and ask without delay.

2 Thou art coming to a King,
Large petitions with thee bring;
For his grace and power are such,
None can ever ask too much.

3 With my burden I begin;
Lord, remove this load of sin!
Let Thy blood for sinners spilt,
Set my conscience free from guilt!

4 Lord, I come to Thee for rest;
Take possession of my breast;
There, Thy blood-bought right maintain.
And, without a rival, reign.
NEWTON.

88.

1 Lord, we come before Thee now;
At Thy feet we humbly bow;
O, do not our suit disdain;
Shall we seek Thee, Lord, in vain?

2 Lord, on Thee our souls depend;
In compassion now descend;
Fill our hearts with Thy rich grace;
Tune our lips to sing Thy praise.

3 Comfort those who weep and mourn;
Let the time of joy return;
Those that are cast down, lift up;
Make them strong in faith and hope.

4 Grant that all may seek and find
Thee a God supremely kind;
Heal the sick; the captive free;
Let us all rejoice in Thee.
HAMMOND.

89.

1 Lord, 'tis sweet to mingle where
Christians meet for social prayer;
O, 'tis sweet with them to raise
Songs of holy joy and praise!

2 From Thy gracious presence flows
Bliss that softens all our woes;
While Thy Spirit's holy fire
Warms our hearts with pure desire.

3 Here we supplicate Thy throne;
Here, Thy pard'ning grace is known,
Here, we learn Thy righteous ways,
Taste Thy love, and sing Thy praise.

4 Thus with prayer and hymns of joy
We the happy hours employ;
Love and long to love Thee more.
Till from earth to heaven we soar.
TURNER.

90.

1 Come! said Jesus' sacred voice,
Come, and make my path your choice:
I will guide you to your home:
Weary wanderer, hither come.

2 Thou, who homeless and forlorn,
Long has borne the proud world's scorn,
Long hast roamed the barren waste,
Weary wanderer, hither haste.

3 Ye who tossed on beds of pain
Seek for ease, but seek in vain;
Ye, by fiercer anguish torn,
In remorse for guilt who mourn:

4 Hither come, for here is found
Balm that flows for every wound!
Peace that ever shall endure,
Rest eternal, sacred, sure.

THE MANSIONS ABOVE.—CONCLUDED.

Saviour will welcome me there (by and by) He will crown me with life

He will fill me with joy, And his garment of love I shall wear.

No. 92.   RATHBUN. 8s & 7s.
Sir John Bowring.   Ithamar Conkey.

1 In the cross of Christ I glory.
  Towering o'er the wrecks of time,
  All the light of sacred story
  Gathers round its head sublime.

2 When the woes of life o'ertake me,
  Hopes deceive and fears annoy,
  Never shall the Cross forsake me;
  Lo! it glows with peace and joy.

3 When the sun of bliss is beaming
  Light and love upon my way,
  From the Cross the radiance stream- [ing,
  Adds new lustre to the day.

4 Bane and blessing, pain and pleas- [ure,
  By the cross are sanctified;
  Peace is there, that knows no meas-
  ure.
  Joys that thought all time abide.

O! THE BELOVED CITY.—CONCLUDED.

EVAN. C. M.

No. 94.   C. WESLEY.

1 Come, Holy Ghost! our hearts inspire,
   Let us thine influence prove;
   Source of the old prophetic fire!
   Fountain of light and love!

2 Come, Holy Ghost! for, moved by thee,
   The prophets wrote and spoke;
   Unlock the truth,—thyself the key;
   Unseal the sacred book.

3 Expand thy wings, celestial Dove!
   Brood o'er our nature's night;
   On our disordered spirits move,
   And let there now be light.

4 God through himself, we then shall know,
   If thou within us shine;
   And sound, with all thy saints below,
   The depths of love divine.

No. 95.   J. NEWTON.

1 In evil long I took delight,
   Unawed by shame or fear,
   Till a new object struck my sight,
   And stopped my wild career.

2 I saw one hanging on a tree,
   In agonies and blood,
   Who fixed his languid eyes on me,
   As near His cross I stood.

3 Sure never, till my latest breath,
   Can I forget that look;
   It seemed to charge me with his death,
   Though not a word He spoke.

4 My conscience felt and owned the guilt;
   And plunged me in despair;
   I saw my sins his blood had spilt,
   And helped to nail Him there.

5 A second look He gave, which said,
   "I freely all forgive;
   This blood is for thy ransom paid;
   I die, that thou may'st live."

6 Thus, while His death my sins displays
   In all its blackest hue,
   Such is the mystery of grace,
   It seals my pardon too.

No. 96. IMMANUEL'S LAND.

A. R. COUSIN.   WM. F. SHERWIN, by per.

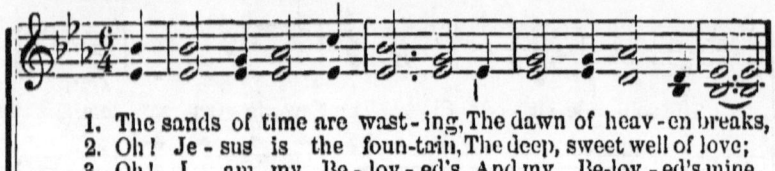

1. The sands of time are wast-ing, The dawn of heav-en breaks,
2. Oh! Je - sus is the foun-tain, The deep, sweet well of love;
3. Oh! I am my Be - lov - ed's, And my Be - lov - ed's mine,

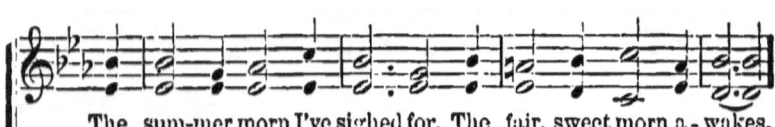

The sum-mer morn I've sighed for, The fair, sweet morn a-wakes.
The streams on earth I've tast-ed, More deep I'll drink a-bove.
He brings a poor vile sin-ner, In - to his house di-vine.

Oh, dark hath been the midnight, But dayspring is at hand,
There to an o-cean ful-ness His mer-cy doth ex-pand.
Up - on the Rock of A - ges, My soul redeemed shall stand,

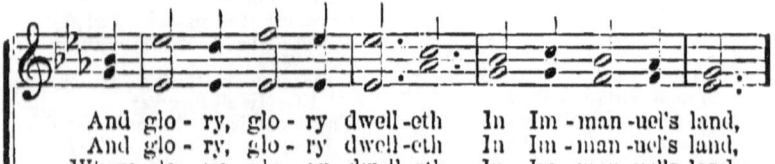

And glo - ry, glo - ry dwell-eth In Im-man-uel's land,
And glo - ry, glo - ry dwell-eth In Im-man-uel's land,
Where glo - ry, glo - ry dwell-eth In Im-man-uel's land,

IMMANUEL'S LAND.—CONCLUDED.

And glo-ry, glo-ry dwell-eth In Im-man-uel's land.

FOREST. L. M.

CHAPIN.

No. 97.

1 O, that my load of sin were gone!
 O, that I could at last submit,
 At Jesus' feet to lay me down,
 To lay my soul at Jesus' feet!

2 Rest for my soul I long to find,
 Fountain of rest, Thou, Saviour, art,
 Give me thy meek and lowly mind,
 And stamp thine image on my heart.

3 Fain would I learn of thee, my God,
 Thy light and easy burden prove;
 The cross, all stained with hallowed
 The labor of Thy dying love. [blood,

4 I would; but Thou must give the
  power;
 My heart from every sin release;
 Bring near, bring near the joyful hour,
 And fill my soul with heavenly peace.

5 Come, Lord, the drooping sinner
  cheer,
 Nor let Thy chariot wheels delay,
 Appear, in my poor heart, appear;
 My God, my Saviour come away.

No. 98.

1 Show pity, Lord; O Lord, forgive;
 Let a repenting rebel live;
 Are not Thy mercies large and free?
 May not a sinner trust in Thee?

2 My crimes, though great, cannot sur-
  pass
 The power and glory of Thy grace;
 Great God, Thy nature hath no bound;
 So let Thy pardoning love be found.

3 O, wash my soul from every sin,
 And make my guilty conscience clean;
 Here, on my heart, the burden lies,
 And past offences pain mine eyes.

4 My lips, with shame, my sins confess,
 Against Thy law, against Thy grace;
 Lord, should thy judgment grow severe,
 I am condemned, but Thou art clear.

5 Yet, save a trembling sinner, Lord,
 Whose hopes still hov'ring round Thy
   word,   [there,
 Would light on some sweet promise
 Some sure support against despair.

STAND UP FOR JESUS.

No. 100. DUFFIELD.

1 Stand up! stand up for Jesus!
 Ye soldiers of the cross;
Lift high His royal banner,
 It must not suffer loss;
From victory unto victory
 His army he shall lead,
Till every foe is vanquished,
 And Christ is Lord indeed.

2 Stand up! stand up for Jesus!
 Stand in His strength alone;
The arm of flesh will fail you—
 Ye dare not trust your own;
Put on the gospel armor,
 And, watching unto prayer,
Where duty calls, or danger,
 Be never wanting there.

3 Stand up! stand up for Jesus!
 The strife will not be long;
This day the noise of battle,
 The next the victor's song.
To him that overcometh
 A crown of life shall be;
He with the King of Glory
 Shall reign eternally.

No. 101. S. F. SMITH.

1 The morning light is breaking;
 The darkness disappears;
The sons of earth are waking
 To penitential tears;
Each breeze that sweeps the ocean
 Brings tidings from afar
Of nations in commotion,
 Prepared for Zion's war.

2 Rich dews of grace come o'er us,
 In many a gentle shower,
And brighter scenes before us
 Are opening every hour:
Each cry, to heaven going,
 Abundant answers brings,
And heavenly gales are blowing,
 With peace upon their wings.

3 See heathen nations bending
 Before the God we love,
And thousand hearts ascending
 In gratitude above;
While sinners, now confessing,
 The gospel call obey,
And seek the Saviour's blessing—
 A nation in a day.

4 Blest river of salvation,
 Pursue thy onward way;
Flow thou to every nation,
 Nor in thy richness stay:
Stay not till all the lowly
 Triumphant reach their home;
Stay not till all the holy
 Proclaim, "The Lord is come."

No. 102.

1 When shall the voice of singing
 Flow joyfully along?
When hill and valley ringing
 With one triumphant song,
Proclaim the contest ended,
 And Him who once was slain,
Again to earth descended,
 In righteousness to reign?

2 Then from the craggy mountains
 The sacred shout shall fly
And shady vales and fountains
 Shall echo the reply.
High tower and lowly dwelling
 Shall send the chorus round,
All hallelujah swelling
 In one eternal sound.

No. 103. HOLY, HOLY! LORD, GOD ALMIGHTY!

HEBER.   Rev. J. B. DYKES.

1. Ho-ly, Ho-ly, Ho-ly! Lord God Al-might-y! Ear-ly in the morning our song shall rise to Thee; Ho-ly, Ho-ly, Ho-ly! Mer-ci-ful and Mighty! God in three Persons, blessed Trin-i-ty.
2. Ho-ly, Ho-ly, Ho-ly! all the saints adore Thee, Casting down their golden crowns around the glassy sea; Che-ru-bim and Seraphim fall-ing down be-fore Thee, Which wert and art, and ev-er-more shalt be.
3. Ho-ly, Ho-ly, Ho-ly! tho' the dark-ness hide Thee, Tho' the eye of sin-ful man Thy glo-ry may not see, On-ly Thou art Ho-ly, there is none be-side Thee Per-fect in power, in love and pu-ri-ty. A-MEN.

4 Holy, Holy, Holy! Lord God Al-
mighty!
All Thy works shall praise thy name
in earth, and sky, and sea;
Holy, Holy, Holy! Merciful and
Mighty!
God in three Persons, blessed
Trinity!   AMEN.

(94)

No. 105. JESUS, I MY CROSS HAVE TAKEN.

HENRY F. LYTE. Air, Mozart. Arr. by H. P. M.

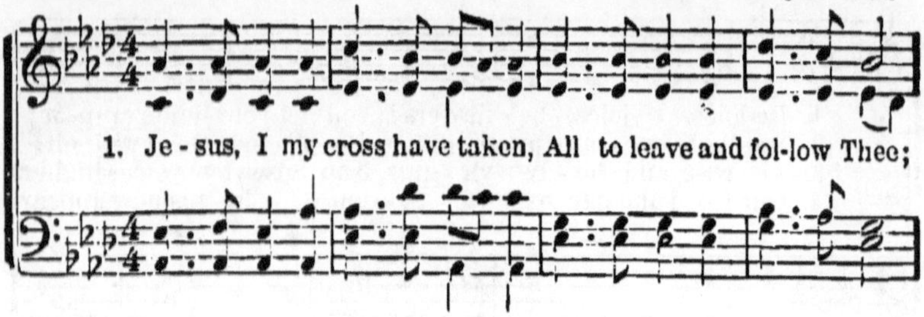

1. Je-sus, I my cross have taken, All to leave and fol-low Thee;
Nak-ed, poor, despised, forsaken, Thou from hence my all shall be.
D. S. Yet how rich is my con-di-tion! God and heaven are still my own.
Per-ish ev-ery fond am-bi-tion, All I've sought, or hoped, or known;

2.
Let the world despise and leave me;
 They have left my Saviour, too;
Human hearts and looks deceive me;
 Thou art not, like them, untrue;
And while thou shalt smile upon me,
 God of wisdom, love, and might,
Foes may hate, and friends may scorn me;
 Show Thy face and all is bright.

3.
Man may trouble and distress me,
 'Twill but drive me to Thy breast;
Life with trials hard may press me,
 Heaven will bring me sweeter rest.

Oh! 'tis not in grief to harm me
 While Thy love if left to me,
Oh! 'twere not in joy to charm me,
 Were that joy unmixed with Thee.

4.
Soul, then know thy full salvation;
 Rise o'er sin, and fear, and care,
Joy to find in every station
 Something still to do or bear.
Soon shall close thy earthly mission,
 Soon shall pass thy pilgrim days:
Hope shall change to glad fruition,
 Faith to sight, and prayer to praise.

(96)

No. 106.   JESUS, LET THY PITYING EYE.

C. WESLEY, 1749.   W. H. OAKLEY.

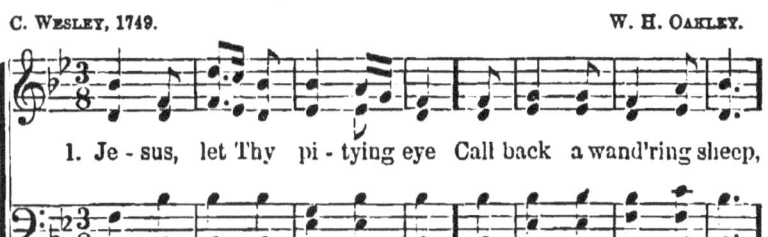

1. Je-sus, let Thy pi-tying eye Call back a wand'ring sheep,

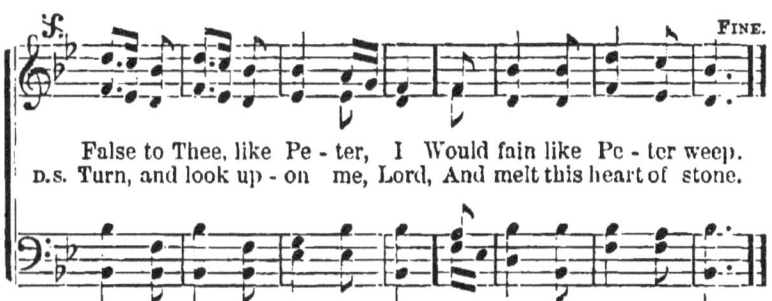

False to Thee, like Pe-ter, I Would fain like Pe-ter weep.
D.S. Turn, and look up-on me, Lord, And melt this heart of stone.

Let me be by grace restored; On me be all long suff'ring shown;

2.
Saviour, Prince, enthroned above,
　Repentance to impart,
Give me, through Thy dying love,
　The humble, contrite heart:
Give what I have long implored,
　A portion of Thy grief unknown;
Turn, and look upon me, Lord,
　And break my heart of stone.

3.
For Thine own compassion's sake,
　The gracious wonder show;
Cast my sins behind Thy back,
　And wash me white as snow;
If Thy bowels now are stirr'd,
　If now I do myself bemoan,
Turn, and look upon me, Lord,
　And break my heart of stone.

MANOAH. C. M.

No. 107.   MISS C. STURTEVANT.

1 O, Lord, my weary soul sustain,
   Uphold me with Thy grace;
 Earth's dearest pleasures are in vain,
   Unless I see Thy face.

2 I hunger for the bread of life,
   I thirst for righteousness;
 My aching spirit worn with strife,
   Yearns for Thy tenderness.

3 Without Thy fond embracing arm,
   I faint, and fall, and die;
 Each shadow fills me with alarm—
   O, hear my plaintive cry.

4 And, when Thou hearest, answer, Lord,
   Abiding peace bestow.
 Then shall I rest upon Thy word,
   And Thy salvation know.

No. 108.   MRS. H. M. WILLIAMS.

1 While Thee I seek, protecting Power,
   Be my vain wishes stilled;
 And may this consecrated hour
   With better hopes be filled.

2 Thy love the power of thought bestowed!
   To Thee my thoughts would soar;
 Thy mercy o'er my life has flowed;
   That mercy I adore.

3 In each event of life, how clear
   Thy ruling hand I see!
 Each blessing to my soul more dear,
   Because conferred by Thee.

4 In every joy that crowns my days,
   In every pain I bear,
 My heart shall find delight in praise,
   Or seek relief in prayer.

5 When gladness wings my favored hour,
   Thy love my thoughts shall fill;
 Resigned, when storms of sorrow lower,
   My soul shall meet Thy will.

6 My lifted eye without a tear
   The gathering storm shall see;
 My steadfast heart shall know no fear,
   That heart shall rest on Thee.

No. 109.   HAWEIS.

1 O Thou from whom all goodness flows
   I lift my soul to Thee;
 In all my sorrows, conflicts, woes,
   O Lord, remember me.

2 When worn with pain, disease, and grief,
   This feeble body see;
 Grant patience, rest, and kind relief;
   O Lord, remember me.

3 When, in the solemn hour of death,
   I wait Thy just decree,
 Be this the prayer of my last breath,
   O Lord, remember me.

4 And when before thy throne I stand,
   And lift my soul to Thee,
 Then, with the saints at Thy right hand,
   O Lord, remember me.

ROCKINGHAM. L. M.
Dr. Lowell Mason.

No. 110.
Wm. Cowper.

1 What various hindrances we meet,
  In coming to the mercy seat !
  Yet who that knows the worth of prayer,
  But wishes to be often there ?

2 Prayer makes the darkened cloud withdraw ;
  Prayer climbs the ladder Jacob saw,
  Gives exercise to faith and love,
  Brings every blessing from above.

3 Restraining prayer, we cease to fight ;
  Prayer makes the Christian's armor bright ;
  And Satan trembles when he sees
  The weakest saint upon his knee.

No. 111.

1 Jesus shall reign where'er the sun
  Does his successive journeys run;
  His kingdom stretch from shore to shore
  Till moons shall wax and wane no more.

2 For him shall endless pray'r be made,
  And endless praises crown his head;
  His name, like sweet perfume, shall rise
  With every morning sacrifice.

3 People and realms of every tongue
  Dwell on His love with sweetest song:
  And infant voices shall proclaim
  Their early blessings on His name.

4 Blessings abound where'er he reigns,
  The joyful prisoner bursts his chains;
  The weary find eternal rest,
  And all the sons of want are blest.

5 Let every creature rise and bring
  Peculiar honors to our King;
  Angels descend with songs again,
  And earth repeat the loud Amen.

No. 112.

1 When I survey the wondrous cross
  On which the Prince of glory died,
  My richest gain I count but loss,
  And pour contempt on all my pride.

2 Forbid it, Lord, that I should boast,
  Save in the death of Christ, my God;
  All the vain things that charm me most
  I sacrifice them to His blood.

3 See, from his head, his hands, his feet,
  Sorrow and love flow mingled down:
  Did e'er such love and sorrow meet,
  Or thorns compose so rich a crown ?

4 Were all the realm of nature mine,
  That were a present far too small;
  Love so amazing, so divine,
  Demands my soul, my life, my all.

No. 113.

1 Stay, thou insulted Spirit, stay,
  Though I have done thee such despite;
  Cast not a sinner quite away,
  Nor take thine everlasting flight.

2 Though I have most unfaithful been
  Of all who e'er thy grace received,
  Ten thousand times thy goodness seen,
  Ten thousand times thy goodness grieved.

3 Yet, O, the chief of sinners spare,
  In honor of my great High Priest;
  Nor, in thy righteous anger swear
  I shall not see thy people's rest.

4 My weary soul, O God, release ;
  Uphold me with Thy gracious hand ;
  O, guide me into perfect peace,
  And bring me to the promised land.

SPANISH HYMN. 7s 6 Lines or Double.

No. 115.

1 PEOPLE of the living God!
  I have sought the world around,
  Paths of sin and sorrow trod,
  Peace and comfort no where found:
Now to you my spirit turns,
Turns,—a fugitive unblest;
Brethren! where your altar burns,
  O receive me into rest.

2 Lonely I no longer roam,
  Like the cloud, the wind, the wave,
  Where you dwell shall be my home,
  Where you die shall be my grave;
Mine the God whom you adore,
Your Redeemer shall be mine;
Earth can fill my soul no more,
  Every idol I resign.

No. 116.

1 JESUS, Shepherd of Thy sheep,
  In Thine arms my spirit keep;
  I am weak, and I am lone,
  Jesus, take me for Thine own.
In Thy bosom Thou dost bear,
Those who most do need Thy care,
I the humblest lamb would be
I would trust myself to Thee.

2 Fair and lovely to behold
  Is Thy lower earthly fold;
  Guardian care shall never fail
  To the flock within its pale.
Still my ardent hopes aspire
To that better home and higher
Where from every fold Thy sheep,
Thou shalt bring and safely keep.

No. 117. SIR R. GRANT.

1 SAVIOUR when in dust to Thee
  Low we bow the adoring knee,—
  When repentant to the skies
  Scarce we lift our streaming eyes,—
O, by all Thy pain and woe
Suffer'd once for man below,
Bending from Thy throne on high
  Hear our solemn litany.

2 By Thine hour of dark despair,
  By Thine agony of prayer;
  By the cross, the nail, the thorn,
  Piercing spear, and tort'ring scorn;
By the gloom that veil'd the skies
O'er the dreadful sacrifice,—
Listen to our humble cry,
  Hear our solemn litany.

3 By Thy deep, expiring groan;
  By the sad sepulchral stone;
  By the vault whose dark abode
  Hold in vain the rising God —
O, from earth to heaven restored
Mighty, re-ascended Lord,
Saviour, listen to our cry,
  Hear our solemn litany.

No. 118.

1 BY Thy birth, and by Thy tears;
  By Thy human griefs and fears;
  By Thy conflict in the hour
  Of the subtle tempter's power—
Saviour, look with pitying eye,
Saviour, help me, or I die.

2 By the tenderness that wept
  O'er the grave where Laz'rus slept;
  By the bitter tears that flow'd
  Over Salem's lost abode—
Saviour, look with pitying eye;
Saviour, help me, or I die.

3 By Thy lonely hour of prayer;
  By the fearful conflict there;
  By Thy cross and dying cries;
  By Thy one great sacrifice—
Saviour, look with pitying eye;
Saviour, help me, or I die.

(101)

No. 119. OH EYES THAT ARE WEARY.

1. O eyes that are wea - ry, and hearts that are sore!
Look off un - to Je - sus, and sor - row no more!
The light of His coun - te - nance shin-eth so bright,
That here, as in heav - en, there need be no night.

2. While look - ing to Je - sus my heart can - not fear;
I trem - ble no more when I feel He is near;
I know that His pres - ence my safeguard shall be,
For, "Why are you troubled?" He saith un - to me.

3. Still look - ing to Je - sus, O may I be found,
When Jordan's dark wa - ters en - com-pass me round:
They bear me a - way in His pres-ence to be:
I see Him still near - er whom al - ways I see.

4. Then, then shall I know the full beau - ty and grace
Of Je - sus, my Lord, when I stand face to face;
Shall know how His love went be - fore me each day,
And won - der that ev - er my eyes turned a - way.

(102)

BALERMA. C. M.

No. 120. REV. EDMOND JONES.

1 Come, humble sinner, in whose breast
A thousand thoughts resolve,
Come, with your guilt and fear oppress'd,
And make this last resolve:

2 I'll go to Jesus, though my sin
Like mountains round me close;
I know his courts, I'll enter in,
Whatever may oppose.

3 Prostrate I'll lie before His throne,
And there my guilt confess;
I'll tell Him I'm a wretch undone
Without His sovereign grace.

4 Perhaps He will admit my plea,
Perhaps will hear my prayer;
But if I perish, I will pray,
And perish only there.

5 I can but perish, if I go—
I am resolved to try;
For if I stay away, I know
I must forever die.

6 But if I die with mercy sought
When I the King have tried,
This were to die, delightful thought,
As sinner never died.

No. 121. REV. J. NEWTON.

1 Approach, my soul, the mercy-seat,
Where Jesus answers prayer;
There humbly fall before His feet,
For none can perish there.

2 Thy promise is my only plea—
With this I venture nigh;
Thou callest burdened souls to Thee
And such, O Lord, am I.

3 Bowed down beneath a load of sin,
By Satan sorely pressed,
By war without, and fears within,
I come to Thee for rest.

4 Be Thou my shield and hiding-place,
That, sheltered near Thy side,
I may my fierce accuser face,
And tell him Thou hast died.

No. 122. HERVEY.

1 Since all the varying scenes of time
God's watchful eye surveys,
O, who so wise to choose our lot,
Or to appoint our ways!

2 Good when he gives,—supremely good,—
Nor less when he denies;
E'en crosses, from his sovereign hand,
Are blessings in disguise.

3 Why should we doubt a Father's love,
So constant and so kind?
To His unerring, gracious will
Be every wish resigned.

4 In Thy fair book of life divine,
My God, inscribe my name:
There let it fill some humble place,
Beneath my Lord, the Lamb.

No. 123. C. WESLEY.

1 My God, I know, I feel Thee mine,
And will not quit my claim,
Till all I have is lost in Thine
And all renewed I am.

2 I hold Thee with a trembling hand
And will not let Thee go,
Till steadfastly by faith I stand,
And all Thy goodness know.

(103)

No. 124. THE HARVEST IS PASSING.

REV. JOHN PARKER.   WM. F. SHERWIN.

1. Why stand ye here idling to-day? There's work in the vineyard for all; The daylight is passing a-way, O, hear ye the vine dresser's call.
2. The Master hath need of thy toil, The harvest is waiting for thee; If idle, thy portion will spoil, O, who would a loi-ter-er be?
3. The resting will soon enough come, And thro' an e-ter-ni-ty last; With shoutings the reapers come home, And toiling for-ev-er be past.
4. From the vineyard of such a dear friend, O, who would in idleness stay? Remember, our la-bor will end In the rest of the great har-vest day.

REFRAIN.

Then rise, brothers, rise to the toil of the day! The harvest of Je-sus is pass-ing away, The har-vest is passing

(104)   Copyright, 1879, by Wm. F. Sherwin.

THE HARVEST IS PASSING.—CONCLUDED.

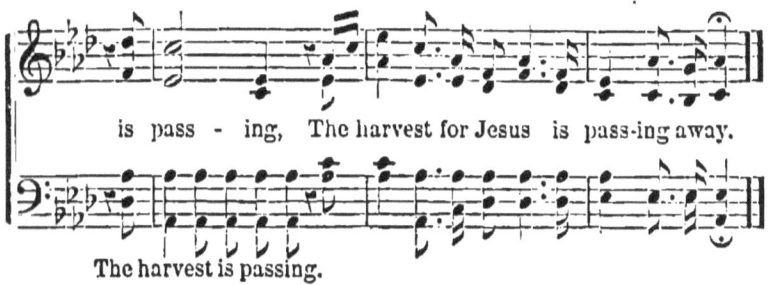

is pass - ing, The harvest for Jesus is pass-ing away.

The harvest is passing.

AMERICA. 6s & 4s.

No. 125.

1 GOD bless our native land!
　Firm may she ever stand,
　　Through storm and night;
　When the wild tempest rave,
　Ruler of wind and wave,
　Do thou our country save
　　By thy great might.

2 For her our prayer shall rise
　To God, above the skies;
　　On him we wait:
　Thou who art ever nigh,
　Guarding with watchful eye,
　To thee aloud we cry,
　　God save the State!

No. 126.　　　　　　　NICOLL.

1 Lord, from Thy blessed throne,
　Sorrow look down upon
　　God save the poor

　Teach them true liberty
　Make them from tyrants free
　Let their homes happy be
　　God save the poor.

2 The arms of wicked men,
　Do Thou with might restrain
　　God save the poor
　Raise Thou their lowliness
　Succor thou their distress
　Thou whom the meanest bless
　　God save the poor.

3 Give them stanch honesty
　Let their pride manly be
　　God save the poor
　Help them to hold the right
　Give them both truth and might
　Lord of all life and light
　　God save the poor.

No. 127. AFTER THE CHRISTIAN'S TEARS.

Words by E. J. X X X

1. After the Christian's tears, After his fights and fears,
After his wea-ry cross, "All things below but loss," What then?
Oh, then, a ho-ly calm, Rest-ing on Je-sus' arm;
Oh, then, a deep-er love For the pure home a-bove.

2 After this holy calm,
This rest on Jesus' arm,
After this deepened love
For the pure home above—
    What then?
Oh, then, hard work for Him,
Immortal souls to win;
Then Jesus' presence near,
Death's darkest hour to cheer.

3 And when the work is done,
When the last soul is won,
When Jesus' love and power
Have cheered the dying hour—
    What then?
Oh, then, the crown is given!
Oh, then, the rest in heaven!
Then life in endless day,
When Death has passed away.

Copyright, 1879, by Theodore E. Perkins.

No. 128. ABIDE WITH ME.

2 Not a brief glance I beg, a parting word;
But as Thou dwell'st with Thy disciples, Lord,
Familiar, condescending, patient, free,
Come, not to sojourn, but abide with me!

3 I need Thy presence every passing hour:
What but Thy grace can foil the tempter's power?
Who like Thyself my guide and stay can be?
Thro' cloud and sunshine, oh, abide with me!

No. 130. EVENING HYMN.

CHARLES F. DEEMS. (*For Family Devotion.*) Harmonized for this work.

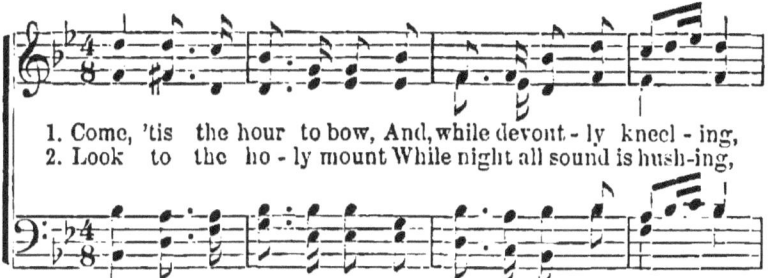

1. Come, 'tis the hour to bow, And, while devout-ly kneel-ing,
2. Look to the ho-ly mount While night all sound is hush-ing,

D. C. *Come, 'tis the hour to bow, And, while devout-ly kneel-ing,*

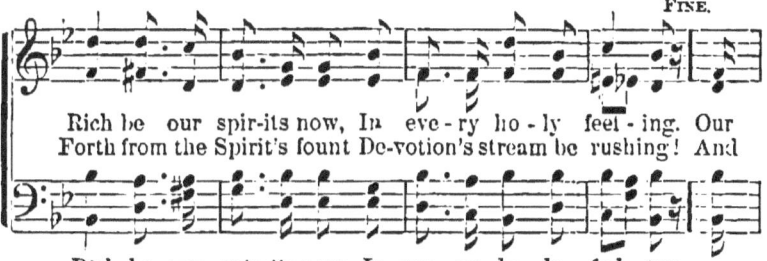

Rich be our spir-its now, In eve-ry ho-ly feel-ing. Our
Forth from the Spirit's fount De-votion's stream be rushing! And

Rich be our spir-its now, In eve-ry ho-ly feel-ing.

joys and tears, our hopes and fears, To heaven be meekly spoken. While
when cold Death shall chill the breath, In which our prayers are swelling,
We'll

faith looks up to Christ our hope, Whose heart for us was bro-ken.
join the hymn of Cher-u-bim, In God's e-ter-nal dwell-ing.

Copyright, 1879, by Theodore E. Perkins.

No. 131.   GLOOMY, STILL GLOOMY.

CHARLES F. DEEMS.   *(Storm Hymn.)*

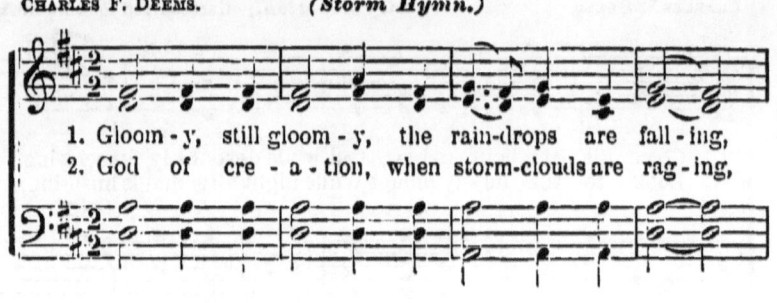

1. Gloom-y, still gloom-y, the rain-drops are fall-ing,
2. God of cre-a-tion, when storm-clouds are rag-ing,

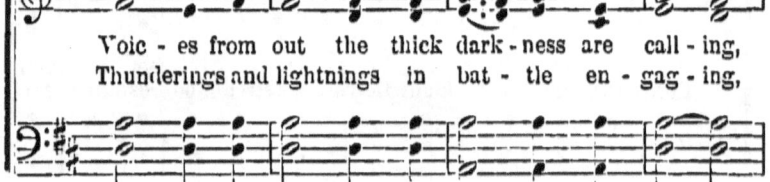

Voic-es from out the thick dark-ness are call-ing,
Thunderings and lightnings in bat-tle en-gag-ing,

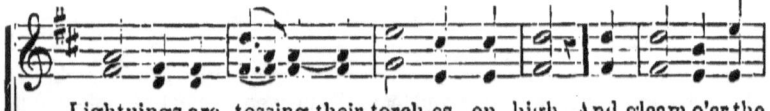

Lightnings are tossing their torch-es on high, And gleam o'er the
Shield Thou our hearts by the wings of Thy love, While gloom mantles

bat-tle-ment-clouds of the sky, While the crash of the
round us, and strife raves a-bove! When our life's lat-est

(110)

GLOOMY, STILL GLOOMY.—CONCLUDE

thun-der doth sol-emn-ly roll, Ac-cents that deepen the awe of the soul. Fa-ther, de-fend us! Father, for-give us! Fa-ther, re-ceive us, Thro' Jesus Christ our Lord! A-MEN.

tem-pest has hushed its a-larms, Gent-ly our spir-its up-bear in Thine arms. Fa-ther, &c.

No. 132.   EVENING HYMN.

1 FADING, still fading, the last beam is shining,
Father in heaven, the day is declining,
Safety and innocence fly with the light,
Temptation and danger walk forth with the night;
From the fall of the shade till the morning bells chime,
Shield us from danger, save us from crime.
 Father, have mercy, Father, have mercy,
Father, have mercy thro' Jesus Christ our Lord.

2 Father in heaven! O hear when we call;
Hear for Christ's sake, who is Saviour of all;
Feeble and fainting we trust in Thy might,
In doubting and darkness Thy love be our light.
Let us sleep on Thy breast while the night taper burns,
Wake in Thy arms when morning returns.
 Father, have mercy. Father, have mercy,
Father, have mercy thro' Jesus Christ our Lord. AMEN.

No. 133. LET JESUS WEAR THE CROWN.

SILAS J. VAIL.

1. I know whatev-er good is mine To Je-sus' grace I owe, That long my steps His love divine Has (Omit.) guarded here be-low. His lengthened mercy I re-view, Tho' chastened by His frown, The glo-ry all to Him is due, Let Je-sus wear the crown.

2. He led me to His mercy-seat, He met my soul in prayer, And showed to me His bleeding feet, Pierced (Omit.) for my ransom there. My spir-it give to love di-vine The glo-ry and renown! No star-ry di-a-dem be mine, Let Je-sus wear the crown.

3 Too oft I've wandered from my King
To claim a royal seat,
Content am I to sit and sing
Crownless before His feet.
Content when I am called to lay
My earthly armor down,
To take the lowest place, and say
Let Jesus wear the crown.

Copyright, 1879, by Theodore E. Perkins

No. 134. PORTUGUESE HYMN. 11s.

1. How firm a foundation, ye saints of the Lord,
Is laid for your faith in His excellent word!
What more can He say than to you He hath said—
You, who unto Jesus for refuge have fled?

2. Fear not; I am with thee; O, be not dismayed:
I, I am thy God, and will still give thee aid;
I'll strengthen thee, help thee, and cause thee to stand,
Upheld by my righteous, omnipotent hand.

3. When through the deep waters I call thee to go,
The rivers of woe shall not thee overflow:
For I will be with thee, thy troubles to bless,
And sanctify to thee thy deepest distress.

4. When through fiery trials thy pathway shall lie,
My grace, all-sufficient, shall be thy supply;
The flame shall not hurt thee: I only design
Thy dross to consume, and thy gold to refine.

5. E'en down to old age, all my people shall prove
My sovereign, eternal, unchangeable love;
And when hoary hairs shall their temples adorn,
Like lambs they shall still in my bosom be borne.

6. The soul that on Jesus hath leaned for repose,
I will not, I will not, desert to his foes;
That soul, though all hell should endeavor to shake,
I'll never, no, never, no, never, forsake.

REV. JOHN KIRKHAM.

I AM FAR FROM THE LAND.—CONCLUDED.

(115)

No. 136. COME UNTO ME, EARTH'S WEARY ONES.
Rev. P. A. Hanaford.

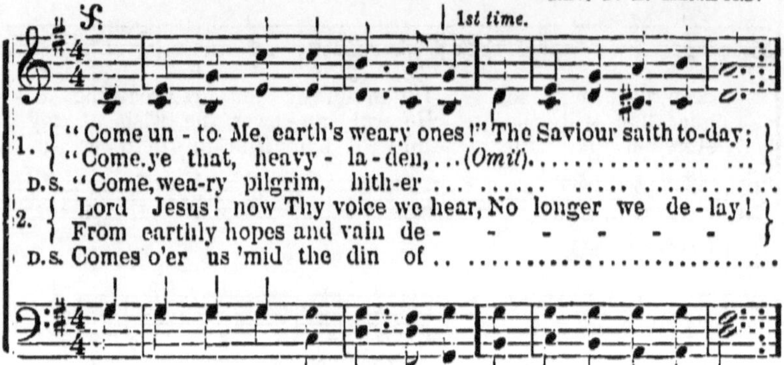

1. { "Come un-to Me, earth's weary ones!" The Saviour saith to-day;
    "Come, ye that, heavy-la-den,...(Omit)................. }
   D.S. "Come, wea-ry pilgrim, hith-er ....

2. { Lord Jesus! now Thy voice we hear, No longer we de-lay!
    From earthly hopes and vain de- - - - - - - }
   D.S. Comes o'er us 'mid the din of ..

sigh, Your burdens cast a-way! Come, in the sul-try heat of
come, And be for-ev-er blest!"
sires, Our spir-its turn a-way. Thy voice, O Teacher, most di-
earth, And stays our wandering feet.

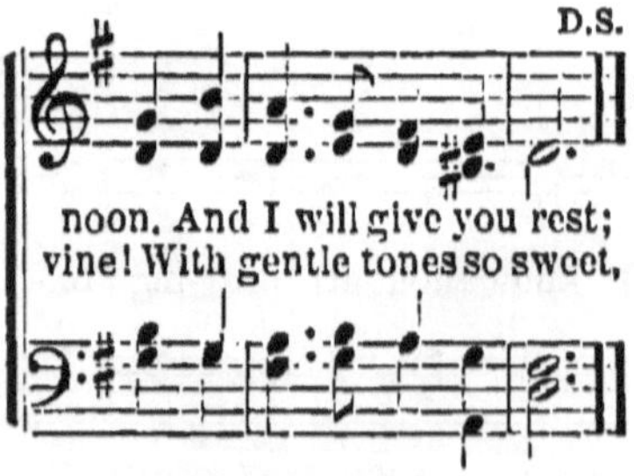

noon. And I will give you rest;
vine! With gentle tones so sweet,

3 Rest, rest in Thee! my spirit longs
For calm and sweet repose;
To have my soul a tranquil lake
Whereon faith's lily grows.
I claim Thy promise, gracious Lord!
Thy love to comfort me,
Repenting, hoping, loving now,
O Christ! I come to Thee.

No. 137. SECOND HYMN.

1 Whatever be our earthly lot,
  Wherever we may roam,
Still to our hearts the brightest spot
Is round the hearth at home:
The home of e'en so lowly birth,
  The hearth by which we sat,
No other spot on all the earth
  Will ever be like that.

2 And when some little trouble weighed
  Upon the childish heart,
Till from our brimming eyes it made
(116) The gushing tear-drops start;

How quick before the genial glow,
  We felt each sorrow cease,
And back the crystal current flow,
  To flood our hearts with peace.

3 And brighter with the passing years
  Seems childhood's sweet employ,
And even sweeter still appears
  Each well-remembered joy;
Around the cheerful hearth at home,
  Where we in childhood sat,
No other spot, where'er we roam,
  Will ever be like that.

ITALIAN HYMN.

No. 138.

1 Come, thou Almighty King,
Help us Thy name to sing,
Help us to praise;
Father all glorious,
O'er all victorious,
Come, and reign over us,
Ancient of Days.

2 Jesus, our Lord, descend;
From all our foes defend,
Nor let us fall;
Let Thine almighty aid
Our sure defence be made,
Our souls on Thee be stayed;
Lord, hear our call.

3 Come, thou incarnate Word,
Gird on thy mighty sword;
Our prayer attend;
Come, and Thy people bless;
Come, give Thy word success·
Spirit of holiness,
On us descend.

4 Come, holy Comforter,
Thy sacred witness bear,
In this glad hour;
Thou, who almighty art,
Now rule in every heart,
And ne'er from us depart,
Spirit of power.

5 To Thee, great One in Three,
The highest praises be,
Hence evermore;
Thy sovereign majesty
May we in glory see,
And to eternity
Love and adore.

No. 139.

1 Glory to God on high!
Let heaven and earth reply,
"Praise ye His name!"
Angels, His love adore,
Who all our sorrows bore;
Saints, sing for ever more,
"Worthy the Lamb."

2 Ye, who surround the throne,
Cheerfully join in one,
Praising His name:
Ye, who have felt His blood
Sealing your peace with God,
Sound through the earth abroad,
"Worthy the Lamb!"

3 Join all the ransomed race,
Our Lord and God to bless:
Praise ye His name.
In Him we will rejoice,
Making a cheerful noise,
Shouting with heart and voice,
"Worthy the Lamb!"

4 Soon must we change our place,
Yet will we never cease
Praising His name:
Still will we tribute bring;
Hail him our gracious king;
And through all ages sing,
"Worthy the Lamb!"

No. 140.

1 Thee, Lord our God alone,
The high and holy One,
Our hearts adore;
Now to the Father raise,
And to the Son, our praise,
And to the Spirit's grace,
Hence, evermore.

No. 141. IN THE SILENT MIDNIGHT WATCHES.

Words by Bishop Coxe.   Music by Geo. F. Sargent.

Moderato with expression.

1. In the si-lent midnight watches, List thy bosom's door,
2. Death comes down with reckless footsteps To the hall and hut,
3. Then 'tis time to stand en-treat-ing Christ to let thee in,

How it knocketh, knocketh, knocketh, Knocketh ev-er-more;
Think you death will tar-ry knocking When the door is shut?
At the gate of heav-en beating, Waiting for thy sin;

(118)   Copyright, 1879, by Geo. F. Sargent.

IN THE SILENT MIDNIGHT WATCHES.—CONCLUDED.

(119)

NOT HALF HAS EVER BEEN TOLD.—CONCLUDED.

riv - er, Clear as crys - tal and pure to be - hold; But not
tor - row, The in - hab - it - ants nev - er grow old; But not
bless - ed, As they walk thro' the streets of pure gold; But not
tect us, If for safe - ty we en - ter His fold; But not

half of that cit - y's bright glo - ry To mor-tals has ev-er been told.
half of the joys that a - wait them To mor-tals has ev-er been told.
half of the won-der - ful sto - ry To mor-tals has ev-er been told.
half of His goodness and mer - cy To mor-tals has ev-er been told.

CHORUS.

Not half has ev - er been told.... Not half has ev-er been told.... Not
been told, been told,

Repeat Chorus pp

half of that cit - y's bright glo - ry To mor - tals has ev - er been told.

NO NIGHT, NO TEARS.—CONCLUDED.

is a world where comes no night, It needs no
If we love Him we shall see That "land from
sun nor moon to light, For Jesus' presence makes it
sin and sorrow free," And oh, we know that there will
bright, No night is there, No night is there.
be No tears there, No tears there.

No. 144. CHILD OF SIN AND SORROW.

1 Child of sin and sorrow,
  Filled with dismay,
Wait not for to-morrow,
  Yield thee to-day:
Heaven bids thee come,
While yet there's room;
Child of sin and sorrow,
  Hear and obey.

2 Child of sin and sorrow,
  Why wilt thou die?
Come while thou canst borrow
  Help from on high:
Grieve not that love
Which from above,
Child of sin and sorrow,
  Would bring thee nigh.

(123)

HAMBURG. L. M.

No. 146.

1 Just as I am, without one plea,
But that Thy blood was shed for me,
And that thou bid'st me come to thee,
O Lamb of God, I come, I come,

2 Just as I am, and waiting not
To rid my soul of one dark blot,
To thee whose blood can cleanse each spot,
O Lamb of God, I come, I come.

3 Just as I am, though tossed about
With many a conflict, many a doubt,
Fightings within, and fears without,
O Lamb of God, I come, I come.

4 Just as I am—poor, wretched, blind;
Sight, riches, healing of the mind,
Yea, all I need, in Thee to find,
O Lamb of God, I come, I come.

5 Just as I am—Thou wilt receive,
Wilt welcome, pardon, cleanse, relieve;
Because Thy promise I believe,
O Lamb of God, I come, I come.

6 Just as I am—Thy love unknown
Hath broken every barrier down;
Now, to be Thine, yea, Thine alone,
O Lamb of God, I come, I come.

DEDHAM. C. M.

No. 147.

1 Father! whate'er of earthly bliss
Thy sovereign will denies,
Accepted at thy throne of grace,
Let this petition rise:—

2 'Give me a calm, a thankful heart,
From every murmur free;
The blessings of Thy grace impart,
And make me live to Thee.

3 Let the sweet hope that thou art mine
My life and death attend:
Thy presence thro' my journey shine,
And crown my journey's end.'

No. 148.   HOLLEY. 7s.   GEO. HEWS.

1 Softly, now, the light of day
  Fades upon my sight away;
  Free from care, from labor free,
  Lord! I would commune with Thee.

2 Soon, for me, the light of day
  Shall forever pass away;
  Then, from sin and sorrow free,
  Take me, Lord! to dwell with Thee.

No. 149.   OLMUTZ. S. M.

1 And can I yet delay
  My little all to give?—
  To tear my soul from earth away,
  And Jesus to receive?

2 Nay, but I yield, I yield!
  I can hold out no more:
  I sink, by dying love compelled,
  And own Thee Conqueror.

3 Though late, I all forsake;
  My friends, my all, resign:
  Gracious Redeemer, take, O take,
  And seal me ever Thine.

4 Come, and possess me whole,
  Nor hence again remove;
  Settle and fix my wavering soul
  With all Thy weight of love.

5 My one desire be this,
  Thy only love to know;
  Freely to yield all other bliss,
  All other good, below.

6 My life, my portion, Thou;
  Thou all-sufficient art;   [now
  My hope, my heavenly treasure,
  Enter and keep my heart.

No. 150.   MONTGOMERY.
1 "Forever with the Lord!"
  Amen! so let it be:
  Life from the dead is in that word—
  'Tis immortality.

2 Here in the body pent,
  Absent from Him, I roam,
  Yet nightly pitch my moving tent
  A day's march nearer home.

3 "Forever with the Lord!"
  Father, if 'tis Thy will,
  The promise of that faithful word
  E'en here to me fulfill.

4 So when my latest breath
  Shall rend the veil in twain,
  By death I shall escape from death,
  And life eternal gain.

5 Knowing as I am known,
  How shall I love that word,
  And oft repeat before the throne,
  "Forever with the Lord!"

No. 151.
1 Lord, at this closing hour
  Establish every heart
  Upon thy word of truth and power,
  To keep us when we part.

2 Peace to our brethren give;
  Fill all our hearts with love;
  In faith and patience may we live,
  And seek our rest above.

3 Through changes bright or drear,
  We would Thy will pursue;
  And toil to spread thy kingdom here,
  Till we its glory view.

(126)

INDEX.

Titles in Small Caps.—First Lines in Roman.

Title/First Line	No.
ABIDE WITH ME	128
AFTER THE CHRISTIAN'S TEARS	127
All hail the power of Jesus' name	1
ALL TO CHRIST I OWE	20
AMERICA. 6s & 4s	125
Am I a soldier of the cross	61
And can I yet delay	149
An open fountain rich and clear	74
Approach my soul the mercy seat	121
ARLINGTON C. M.	61
ARISE MY SOUL, ARISE	79
AROUND THE CROSS	74
BALERMA. C. M.	120
BATTLING FOR THE LORD	47
BEYOND THE SMILING AND THE	31
Bleet be the tie that binds	53
BOYLSTON. S. M.	69
BRIGHTLY GLEAMS OUR BANNER	64
Brother take thy cross and bear it	15
By thy birth and by thy tears	118
CHILD OF SIN AND SORROW	144
CLING CLOSE TO THE ROCK	35
CLOSE TO THEE	10
Come every soul by sin oppress'd	67
Come Holy Ghost	94
Come humble sinner	120
COME O COME WITH THY BROKEN	40
Come my soul thy suit prepare	87
Come, said Jesus sacred Voice	90
Come thou Almighty King	138
Come thou fount of every blessing	65
Come, 'tis the hour to bow	130
Come to Jesus	7
Come to Jesus to-day	7
COME UNTO ME EARTH'S WEARY ONES	136
COME UNTO ME	114
Come weary wand'rer to the dear	52
CORONATION	1
CROSS AND CROWN	59
Dear Jesus I long to be perfectly	33
Dear Saviour all I think or do	84
DEDHAM. C. M.	147
DENNIS. S. M	53
DEPTH OF MERCY	85
EVAN. C. M	94
EVENING HYMN	130
EVEN ME	13
Fade, fade each earthly joy	36
Fading still fading	132
Father whate'er of earthly bliss	147
FOREST. L. M	97
Forever with the Lord	150
Full of sin though I may be	145
GATHERING HOME	44
GIVE YOURSELF TO JESUS WHOLLY	82
Gloomy, still Gloomy	131
Glory to God on high	139
God bless our native land	125
God loved the world of sinners lost	23
HAMBURG. L. M.	146
Hear us from Thy throne above	43
HOLLEY. 7s	148
HOLY, HOLY LORD GOD ALMIGHTY	103
HOME OF THE SOUL	29
HORTON. 7s	87
How bright that blessed hope	14
How firm a foundation	134
I AM COMING, LORD	9
I am coming to the Cross	5
I AM FAR FROM THE LAND	135
I am glad that I've heard about	4
I AM PRAYING FOR YOU	68
I AM TRUSTING LORD IN THEE	5
I AM WAITING BY THE RIVER	72
I CHOOSE TO FOLLOW JESUS	129
I CLING TO THEE	81
I have a Saviour	68
I have read of a beautiful city	142
I hear the Saviour say	20
I hear Thy welcome voice	9
I know whatever good is mine	133
I LOVE TO TELL THE STORY	48
I SHALL NOT WANT	41
I WILL NEVER LEAVE THEE	28
I will sing you a Song	29
IMMANUEL'S LAND	96
I'M KNEELING AT THE DOOR	21
I'm kneeling Lord at mercy's gate	21
In evil long I took delight	95
In the cross of Christ I glory	92
In the house of my Father above	91
IN THE MANSIONS OF OUR FATHER	99
In some way or other the Lord will	16
IN THE PRESENCE OF THE KING	32
IN THE SILENT MIDNIGHT WATCHES	141
ITALIAN HYMN	138
JESUS I AM WAITING NOW	56
JESUS I MY CROSS HAVE TAKEN	105
JESUS IS HERE	25
JESUS IS MINE	36
JESUS LET THY PITYING EYE	106
JESUS LOVER OF MY SOUL	55
JESUS MY ALL	22
JESUS MY LORD	38

INDEX.

Title	No.
Jesus of Nazareth passeth by	50
Jesus then I know	17
Jesus Thy name I love	38
Jesus will come	14
Jesus will welcome me	80
Jesus Saviour hear our cry	8
Jesus shall reign where'er the Sun	111
Jesus Shepherd of Thy sheep	116
Just as I am, without one plea	146
Keep on praying	24
Laban. S. M	51
Laud ahead, its fruits are waving	63
Lead me on	30
Let Jesus wear the crown	133
Let us gather up the sunbeams	58
Looking unto Jesus	26
Long my spirit pined in sorrow	24
Lord at this closing hour	151
Lord at Thy mercy seat	22
Lord from Thy blessed throne	126
Lord I hear of showers of blessings	13
Lord 'tis sweet to mingle where	89
Lord we come before Thee now	88
Love of Jesus	3
Manoah. C. M	107
Make room for Jesus	39
More love to Thee	12
Must Jesus bear the cross alone	59
My faith looks up to Thee	77
My God I know I feel Thee mine	123
My soul be on Thy guard	51
My spirit in hope is rejoicing	80
Nearer the Cross	46
Nettleton	65
Nearer, my God to Thee	78
No night, no tears	143
Not all the blood of beasts	69
Not half has ever been told	142
Not now my Child	96
Nothing but a contrite heart	145
Nothing but leaves	34
O come to Jesus now	25
O Holy Saviour	81
O land of rest for Thee I sigh	37
O Lord my weary soul sustain	107
O sometimes the shadows are deep	54
O that my load of sin were gone	97
O the beloved City	93
O think of the home over there	60
O thou from whom all goodness flows	109
O to be over yonder	32
O ye that are weary	71
Oh eyes that are weary	119
Oh how he loves	57
Oh to be ready	2
Olmutz. S. M	149
One there is above all others	57
On the cross	66
Onward Christian Soldiers	18
Only Trust Him	67
Pass not by	8
People of the living God	115
Portuguese Hymn	134
Rathbun. 8s & 7s	92
Rejoice and be glad	6
Rejoice, rejoice believers	104
Rest in the shadow of the Rock	62
Rest pilgrim rest	62
Revive us again..(2d Hymn)	6
Rockingham. L. M	110
Rock of Ages	49
Safe within the vail	63
Saviour I follow on	73
Saviour when in dust to Thee	117
Scatter seeds of kindness	58
Show pity Lord, O Lord forgive	98
Since all the varying scenes of time	122
Spanish Hymn	115
Softly now the light of day	148
Stand up for Jesus	100
Stay thou insulted Spirit, Stay	113
Sun of my Soul	42
Take thy Cross	15
Tell me more about Jesus	4
The blessed Saviour died for me	66
The gate ajar for me	27
The harvest is passing	124
The home over there	60
The Lord will provide	16
The mansions above	91
The morning light is breaking	101
The rock that is higher	54
The sands of time are wasting	96
Thee, Lord our God alone	140
There is a fountain filled	11
There is a gate that stands ajar	27
There is a land	83
There is no love like the love of	3
They're gath'ring homeward from	44
Thine eye can see	84
Thine forever	43
Thou my everlasting portion	10
'Tis sweet to think as night comes on	143
To day	45
To-day the Saviour calls	45
To Thee most holy light	75
Trav'ling to the better land	30
Weary not my brother	26
We praise Thee O God..(2d Hymn)	6
We'll wait till Jesus comes	37
We've listed in a holy war	47
What a Friend we have in Jesus	19
What means this eager anxious	50
What various hindrances we meet	110
Whatever be our earthly lot	137
When I survey the wond'rous cross	112
When my sins as mountains rise	28
When my soul within	17
When shall the voice of singing	102
While Thee I seek protecting power	108
Whiter than snow	33
Why not tell Jesus all	52
Why, sinner why	76
Why stand ye here idling to-day	124
Why wilt thou not relent	76
Wondrous love	23